PAUL NEWMAN
& KARAMPAL SINGH

TELLING IT LIKE IT IS
Messages from Beyond

Linda Stein-Luthke
Martin F. Luthke, Ph.D.

Expansion Publishing

PAUL NEWMAN
& KARAMPAL SINGH

TELLING IT LIKE IT IS
Messages from Beyond

Linda Stein-Luthke
Martin F. Luthke, Ph.D.

Copyright © 2012 by Linda Stein-Luthke & Martin F. Luthke
Cover photo © AP/Aynsley Floyd, photographer

ISBN 978-0-9656927-9-3

Expansion  Publishing

11872 Chillicothe Rd. - Chesterland, OH 44026
USA

Table of Contents

Foreword

Dear Reader,

This new book is part of a series of publications that came out of an agreement made prior to embodiment in this lifetime. My husband, Martin and I have been collaborating for close to twenty years now. In that time we have learned many lessons from the Ascended Masters and other beings of Light who have chosen to be connected with us as we've fulfilled our agreement to share their wisdom and guidance.

This book is different from the other books we have offered so far. Paul Newman and Karampal Singh are not part of the Ascended Masters, nor do they belong to the beings of Light that have worked with us before in writing our books. They are, instead, close associates of ours who are also benefiting from the *Ascended Masters* and beings of Light with whom we have been collaborating.

Paul Newman and Karampal Singh have communicated their desire to describe their experiences and insights since moving on to the higher frequencies of Light. It's been a true inspiration to hear another perspective on what is possible for us while we are still on Mother Earth — and what we can choose to experience once we transition to the higher planes.

The information that Paul and Karampal are offering in this book appears to resonate with many. We hope you enjoy reading this book as much as we've enjoyed writing it. The information seems useful and compelling.

Paul Newman needs no further introduction. The first conscious communication with Paul Newman occurred shortly after he passed away from cancer about three years ago. I'd been driving through his old neighborhood in Shaker Heights, Ohio which was also my old neighborhood, and I felt his presence very strongly there. I assumed he was revisiting childhood haunts, which is not unusual for the recently departed. In addition to sharing the same childhood neighborhood, albeit twenty years apart, I had made friends with a friend of his who'd taught at Kenyon College and spent time with Paul when he'd return to his Alma Mater for guest appearances.

So, I did feel a bit of a connection with him, although it didn't seem strong enough for the events that followed.

That day, about three years ago, as I drove past the street where he had lived, we "connected" energetically. Paul was attracted to the Light and the beings of Light who are with us constantly, and he came near me to see what this Light was and to see if he could find out more about it. He then realized I was thinking of him, and became aware that we could consciously communicate. So, he stayed with me to see if we could connect for more than a fleeting thought.

When first he spoke to me he complained how hard it was to get past a group of dearly departed that block me from receiving unwanted visitors from the other planes. He dubbed my father, Martin's father, and other family members and friends "The Lions at the Gate" who guard me well. I've kept the name, even though it was said with sardonic wit, because it fits my higher-plane companions well.

An amazing series of communications followed, some of which made it into a newsletter. Paul led me to understand that he was moving quickly into the Light. He'd done quite a bit of work prior to his departure to be ready for the tasks he would assume from the higher planes. He'd resolved a great deal of karma and was ready to share his advice and wisdom.

Karampal Singh, however, is not exactly a household name. Martin and I have a very close and personal relationship with Karampal Singh not only in this lifetime, but eternally. We are from the same original spark of Light from Infinite Source, then split into three parts instead of the usual two, manifesting as two Yang and one Yin energy. The term often used to describe our relationship is Twin Flame. More information regarding our relationship and history can be found in my autobiography, AGREEMENTS[1].

Even prior to Karampal's transition we were often in contact with him on the higher planes. He lived in India and we were living in the United States at that time, but this did not impede our energetic connection. During his lifetime we also visited with him in India several times.

During his last hours, his children called to inform us that he was nearing the end of his life; we sat in meditation and helped him cross over. Our connection with him became instantly filled with a glorious Light as he left his physical form

[1] For details, please visit www.expansionpublishing.com.

and was fully engulfed in his Light. Ever since we have been even more profoundly connected with him. The impediments and distractions of human life no longer interfere with his connection to us — but we are still prone to being distracted by daily life in our connection with him! So when Paul suggested that this book be a joint collaboration with K.P. — his nickname from his last embodiment — we were only too happy to consent.

Many Blessings of Love and Light,

Linda and Martin

Chapter 1

Paul Newman on the End of Suffering

Hello Linda!

I appreciate your taking the time to indulge my request. It has been a long time by your standards since we've consciously connected, although while you've been sleeping, we've been part of the same group receiving instruction and teachings from these magnificently gorgeous beings of Light that I hooked in with on that day when you were driving through my old neighborhood. Evidently we belong to the same "club" because they were only too ready to greet me and enfold me in their magnificent Light and knowledge.

The amazing thing about this knowledge is that it doesn't arrive so much in words, but is a fantastic "hum" – yep, *AUM* is a good word for it – for this overwhelming Love and the powerful, amazing sound frequencies that fill you up in the most beautiful way. No, there aren't enough words to describe it. But as soon as I hooked into it, I was literally hooked and didn't want to walk away from it again. As wonderful as my life on Earth was, and it was wonderful – marrying Joanne and having so much fun while being able to do so much to help others – I had never known a moment on Earth that was as wonderful as what I was now experiencing on these other realms of consciousness. That's your term I'm using here.

You know what this feels like. You let yourself go enough to feel it often enough and you know it's what keeps you sane there now while the world is going so crazy. It is crazy there now, isn't it?

So what are you doing to help there? You are sharing these messages from these guys here, and yet people still don't believe and understand what you are telling them, do they? That's why I suggested [in a separate communication] you now offer a workshop on what you call the *Fourth Dimension*[2] as a way to get through to folks about what is available to them now. If you understand what I am talking about here, why can't they? Why are you keeping it such a secret? I frequently talk with your father, your husband's father, and your other guides and teachers about how to get the word out, how to share this great news of what you know about and try to share with others. And yet it seems to be such a secret still.

This is the frustrating part about being here. So few of you there are willing to tune in and understand what you can experience **while you are there.** You don't have to wait until you get here to do this. You know this. They don't know it yet. But they should.

It is so awfully important to share this, to share what you know.

People are afraid of the Light there. Did you know that?

---

2   Please refer to *Navigating the Fourth Dimension* published by Expansion Publishing; www.expansionpublishing.com.

I was. I didn't understand it. I thought it was religious bull crap and wanted nothing, absolutely nothing to do with that. But I understand now because you drove through Shaker Heights that day which made me curious and I had to see what the fuss was all about. You leave quite a trail!

I can help you, you know — if you'll let me. That's why I'm here now. To help folks like you. You're spread apart, but you are there. Your partner, Martin is one of them too. We are working hard here to help you there.

That's our job now. To spread the word that this whole friggin planet is moving up and out of the chaos and despair that has plagued it for so long. And you are part of the team moving it up and out. Yep, that's why you are there. And that's why I am here. I'm done with the human job I had to do. And it was a good job. I enjoyed it for the most part. But there is much more to do from here and you are part of that from where you are now. You are not done, kid. Hell, you've got a loooong way to go. That doesn't make you happy, does it? I know you want to be here. But, and this is important, **you are here too**. You, and a lot of folks like you are multi-dimensional. You skate around all the time. Very nimble, too. I know you feel your human body is weak, but you should see how that all looks from here! Extraordinary.

So, get to work there. Tell your old man to sit down and listen to me. I've got lots to tell him too. [...] I don't want to be done talking with either one of you. Please let me in now...

The next day....

I just care that you get the word out about all the change that is happening on Earth. You know we can see it all very clearly. We are not far away in some fantastic place just counting the clouds as they roll by the way people think of "heaven." It isn't like that at all, unless you expect the "harps and angels scene." If you do expect that, it is what you will get. But if you don't really know what to expect, then you actually are open to a really fantastic experience that exceeds anything your human minds can grasp. Indescribable.

But what is describable is the pain we still can sense that so many of you choose to experience, as I did, because you are walking around blindly with absolutely no idea how all the crap you are experiencing is truly unnecessary. It just doesn't need to be that way. You are all blind to so much that I can see now. And hell, yeah! I'm anxious to share what I see. Hey, I know! Can we write a book? [...] Nothing but pure fun as I tell you how great it is here and how all of you can feel great, too, if you want to.

This suffering business has got to end. You are on the last final phase of that. And yeah, you've been saying to let the Light in. That's all folks need to do. But nobody really trusts this, right? Not even you all the time, right? But that's gotta end. And it will. It will. Honest to God it will. It's happening right now. Right now. So, go for it. Trust that gorgeous Light. It's beyond description. You give it colors and tell people to breathe it in. But just get drenched in it. Soak it up. You'll all feel better immediately. Hell, I wish I could have bottled this and put it on a shelf. I'd call it "Newman's Own" and put a halo on my head. That would sell out so fast, it would make you all millionaires in an instant!

But you can carry it around inside you instead and just share it as you move about. You do that now. No bottle, no packaging. Easily accessible to everyone without charge.

Free of charge. Free. That's all you need to do. Just as you've been saying: Breathe it in and let it flow through you and come out of you everywhere. Then everyone and everything you touch gets to feel it, too. It's so easy to spread once you know how to let it in and let it out.

You can all have this now. *All* of you. No need to wait until you get here. I think that about sums it up for now. We'll talk some more.

•• •• ••

Chapter 2

It is Time to Re-Create Your Dream

From Linda:

The idea of writing another book is disconcerting. But yet I find I can't stop. Earlier this week the phone and computer went out. And now the television is misbehaving. I know this is a sign that I am to go within and do the inner work I intended to do. But I can't even sit in my chair and do this properly!

I've been re-reading our book *Navigating the Fourth Dimension* to see why I thought this was the best book that the *Ascended Masters* have channeled through so far, and I see that it does seem to contain everything, so why do I need to channel more?

And how can K.P. and Paul work together? What do they possibly have in common? K.P. lived his life in relative obscurity in India while pursuing deep spiritual awakening and meeting the needs of his family. His life was difficult and stressful.

I don't really know that much about Paul Newman's life outside of what's been written or what I've seen in interviews, but I don't think it was anything like what K.P. experienced. So where is the connection? This all is very puzzling to me that Newman would suggest that he and K.P. could write a book together. I'm sitting here at the computer to get some questions answered.

From Paul:

Okay, so here's the long and short of it. It's very simple. First off, Karampal, (sorry just can't call him K.P. the way he looks here) and I aren't anything like you knew us there. The change comes pretty quickly once you shed the body. He looks pretty robust. Not at all the frail man you knew. Turban is off. He's quite dazzling actually. We don't really need anything that looks like a body now. That's just to keep you happy and something that enables you to recognize us when you see us. Then we usually take on a costume, (kind of like when I was acting) so you can feel comfortable around us when you connect with us here. But we are all, just as you've heard, basically Light. Well, you are Light, too. But you've made an agreement with your environment there to have a part of you take on very tactile forms and live in a tactile setting.

You know, when you're dreaming everything looks very real and you get all caught up in what you are experiencing in your dream. But when you wake up, it all disappears. All you are left with is the memory of it and any emotions you might have attached to that dream experience. That's kind of how we see all of the Earth experience. It's a dream that we wake up from when we leave our bodies and enter this Light-filled place that ultimately seems more real than what we experienced on Earth. We look back on those lives and wonder how we got all caught up in that world just as you often wonder how you got so emotional about your dreams. What's real then?

This is! More real than anything you've ever experienced there. And you can go on about all the terrible, awful things that happen there. We know that when people are suffering and dying it is terrible. We do see it and know it. It is a nightmare for so many. Not a good dream. A terrible dream. Just terrible.

When we were alive, it seemed to go on forever. One of the things Karampal and I do have in common is that we chose to look at the suffering from a very close perspective. And we wondered why we personally didn't have to go through the terrible things that others were experiencing. We both did all we could to help others. We didn't want to see the world stay in such a terrible state, but the problems seemed overwhelming. The world that is living on that beautiful planet that is spinning around in space doesn't seem to have any idea how to solve its problems. It is becoming even more of a nightmare for so many. So many.

Karampal and I and all the others with whom you are connected see this. And we are part of this immense team here that is seeking to help you to **understand that this enormous suffering is about to end.**

We understand that it can't go on as it has. It *must* change. And you are all there to help it change as you learn the tricks of the trade that we now completely understand since we've let go of that dream that we called *life on Earth.*

It is such a disparity to be residing in your physical bodies on this amazingly beautiful planet and see how so many people are seeking to destroy and ruin it. We can still observe that from here. But we can also see the trajectory that your planet is on to correct its own course and solve its own problems.

The planet is lifting itself out of the darkness of the suffering and into the radiant Light. You are there to help make that happen.

You've heard the guidance of these amazing Light forms tell you repeatedly what you can do to help create this transformation. And yet, every day you get distracted by everything that you want to call a problem, or work, or necessity.

You end up thinking: "If I don't do this work, or tackle this problem, then I can honestly project that my life will be terrible and I will add to the suffering I see all around me." You know about these "if-then" sentences. You heard about all of that when you channeled the guy you call *St. Germain*.

This is what killed Karampal. He couldn't reconcile what he felt when he connected to the Light with all the demands of his daily life.

Well, I didn't have that problem. Everything that I touched turned to gold. I did live in a different dream from Karampal that way. What got me all messed up is when the people around me couldn't live the same way. When they would get all confused and miserable because they were caught in that confusion. I hated that. Lost my son that way. That's the stuff that killed me.

I'm not a worrier. Never was. Life just kept going my way. But everyone else worried and got miserable enough to take care of that department so that all I dealt with was the fallout from everyone else's worries. That's what I kept trying to fix. I wanted everyone else's life to be easier. That's what I'm still working on from here. Karampal and I do have that in common.

Karampal got caught in the "worry trap" too. And you do too, Linda. Your life has had its challenges. Everyone goes through that there. But you know that everything has come more easily to you than to most folks. You've had one success in life after another. Why does that happen for some folks and not for others?

That was my big question when I was alive. Never figured it out. I was no saint. Hadn't done anything that I could see that made it possible for all that stuff to come to me. But it did. I wanted some things, sure. But everything I ever wanted, I got. Everything. Then I'd get more.

But now I see that this all had something to do with what you call karma. And that what I did there to get myself so well known was only the beginning of the work I was really going to do. Which is what I am doing here, in this Light from this place. I'm going to do more here, because I can, than I ever did there. Ever. I can be everywhere, all the time. Really spread myself out now. Kinda like when I'd make a movie and many people could watch it all over the world. That was pretty neat. Just like this. You do that with your books. That's how you spread yourself around, with all your writing. You want to do it that way, and I want to help you do it that way.

Have we got a deal? I'm asking you again, but I'm still not seeing that you completely believe this. But come on already! Believe it!

You know, life really does go by in a flash, when you consider this idea of eternity. People on earth are so busy measuring things. How old are you? How long have you done something? How long does it take to get somewhere? How tired will you be at the end of the day?

No one ever stops to realize that you've all been around forever and will continue to exist forever and that the dream you are living in now is but a few blinks of an eye in the grander scheme of all existence. Hell, they think they know how long the earth has been around. Billions of years they say. Hah! They don't even have that right. And the "humans" on it? Well, that's been a few seconds. That's all. Yet, you and everyone and everything else belong to a **huge** conglomerate that keeps creating and recreating itself in the most amazing ways.

What we are telling you to do there is **start that re-creating process now!** Be part of what's making it all happen. Take this whole creation and move it to where it is going. Be part of it. Don't resist. Assist.

•• •• ••

Chapter 3

Karampal on Collaborating with Paul

From Linda:

Well, I've asked a few trusted friends to take a look at what's come through so far, and the response has been positive. I've been encouraged to keep going, so I am. I'm very curious to hear from K.P. (Karampal, according to Paul.) How does he feel about sharing this book with Paul? I know he's been anxious for me to write about him since he's transitioned. He is Martin's and my Twin Flame. And the connection there is very profound. Here comes Paul, something of an interloper, wanting to share what he's learned since he crossed over. Come to think of it, they both left the Earth at about the same time; they probably met up pretty quickly after leaving here. That's interesting to think about, too.

So, K.P., are you there? Do you have a perspective on all of this?

From Karampal:

My darling Linda, of course I am here. As you well know, I am always with you and Martin. We are permanently connected. All the guidance you have received about re-reading *Yogananda* and about the life of *Gandhi* has come from me so that you can keep the Indian perspective fresh in your mind as you look at what is happening in the world. It is helpful when you address my children as well. [...] All the help you do give the children as they learn to stand on their own is deeply appreciated.

All the help you give to so many is deeply appreciated. As our friend, Paul has said, your good deeds and kindness have not gone unnoticed. And yet we know you do not do this for acclaim, but simply because you see your work as what you have agreed to do. Now, I know you wish to take time to be with your children there. What can I offer you before you depart?

Am I willing to work with Paul in collaboration on a book regarding the true nature of reality? For I believe that is the direction we are going in. Many have written such books through the centuries, but Paul believes that using his notoriety may bring a greater readership. I heartily concur in this regard. We both have much to offer and get along well here. There is simply not the animosity, jealousies, and other unpleasant factors that can mar a relationship on the Earth plane. We are all immersed in this loving Light in every moment and so feel no need to go to other means for self-gratification.

There is so much struggle there to find a way to feel good about oneself. Here, one's Self takes over and this profound connection to this unconditionally loving Light erases all need for other efforts to be made. It is a wonderful way to be and one we hope to aid you in experiencing for yourself and sharing with others.

Ah, there is so much more that we are both eager to share with you! Don't be worried or afraid that we will overwhelm you. Your "Lions at the Gate" won't allow that to occur. So be with your darling children and your wonderful Martin.

Know we are drenching you in our love as you move along. You share that love freely with so many. Know it is received and appreciated in every instant.

Much Love, always, Karampal

•• •• ••

Chapter 4

Paul: Remember the "Force"

From Linda:

Many days have passed since last I sat at the computer to let more information come through from Paul and K.P. Part of what has kept me away — aside from the distractions of daily life — is that Martin and I had to work through some challenging karmic entanglements between us and these needed to be addressed and healed before we could collaborate on another book. Relationships must be nurtured continuously for everyone and that includes Martin and me as well.

Additionally, there are many changes occurring on our planet. Mother Nature has responded to the challenges presented to her by humanity, and earthquakes, floods, droughts, tornadoes, and hurricanes are rampant right now. North America has received an exceptional number of challenges this year [2011]. Since that continent is my home and we have many family members over there the recent events have been particularly distracting.

Meanwhile, Paul has been coming to me with a *James Taylor-song* that I love entitled *Whenever I See Your Smiling Face*. This does get my attention and he follows up with entreaties that I continue to do this writing with him.

Why *James Taylor?* Because he knows I adore his music and this song especially. He's trying to make his bothersome behavior appealing. And it's working! I'm at the computer, and I'm typing away. Martin and I are healing our issues and continually asking for healing for our planet. And now it's time to get to work....

From Paul:

Hi Linda!

I'm here. You are working at the computer again. That's great. You know, I was never a big fan of all this electronic stuff, but I can see how it's been helpful in getting the word out. So it's got its good uses and then I've seen lots of folks abuse this just as they abuse all kinds of things to distract themselves from accepting the true reality.

I know I immersed myself in distractions as well because I didn't know any better. Anything with an engine and wheels was far more appealing to me than anything else I did. Now, I know better and see that I wasted a lot of time. But the guys here don't think that's true. See, they don't think anything we do is a mistake, actually. They think it was all right and perfect for us to grow and learn. Everything is a lesson to teach us one thing: That no matter what we try to do while we are alive, if it's not helping us wake up and learn there is more than just all that third-dimensional stuff, then we will never find the satisfaction that we seek out of life.

I've had the greatest of everything. Everything. And yeah, there was satisfaction for a while. But then I wanted more. I always wanted more. Joanne could never understand that. Women have it easier, I think, because they have to feel a God-energy and develop a sense of the miracle of creation when they have children. I never felt that the same way *Joanne* did. Hell, I didn't always know which screw was the one that made the kid! And then I was done; my job was over and I could move on. But when you have to carry a kid around for nine months inside you and then take care of it forever, you've got to change. I didn't have to do any of that. In my day, it was even easier for the guy to walk away and leave that to the woman to do.

Now, it seems in some places women make the men do more. But I was never up for any of that nonsense. I wanted my freedom because I thought that meant more. I did help people. That was important to me. But nothing ever gave me the satisfaction that I think Joanne felt in raising our kids. I helped there too. But that was mainly her job. And she did a great job. They are great kids. Could I have helped more? Absolutely. But I didn't understand about creating life, or wonder where it all came from. I questioned it a bit, but I never really tried to understand.

But I do get it now. And what I see is amazing from here. You've got a ringside seat on your planet to the most glorious creation of life there on that little blue ball and most of you don't get it. You don't get it all. Everything you see that makes that planet tick and keep life going is just amazing from here.

You see, it all begins with a thrust of energy — a Force that most of you can't even begin to appreciate because you'll want to call it God and put it in a box that you'll call religion and give it all these good and bad connotations.

Nothing could be farther from the truth. Any idea that you have of something called a "God" limits what this is. It's beyond anything you can imagine.

It is so *huge*. So amazing and yes, it is glorious. And it created you and everything you see. Yet, on any given day you all think you know more and are smarter, stronger, and more powerful than this Force.

It's amazing how many people I dealt with who, including myself, thought that we were the "bees knees." We thought we were just wonderful. Hell, I was gorgeous, talented, and brilliant. That's what everybody told me. And I believed my own press. Why not? How could anything including this "God" that I didn't understand, be better than me?

But this thing I'll call a "Force" has helped me see that in the greater scheme of things I'm no more important than a grain of sand on a beach. In fact, sand is comprised of the same energy that went into creating me! We all come from this "Force" and when we know that, then we can be as powerful as this "Force" in fixing up everything on the planet, including the grains of sand on the beaches.

Conversely, when we ignore the "Force" and don't let ourselves open up to it, we can mess things up pretty good for our planet. Which is what you are looking at now.

So, our job here is to help you there to see that you need to hang out with this "Force" and let it show you how to clean up the mess you've created there.

I'm part of that team now. And Linda is finally listening enough *(she likes James Taylor!),* so that I can help her help you all.

To really get started, you want to wonder how it all began. Well, the answer to that is, I don't know. It doesn't seem to have a beginning. It seems to have always existed. It seems to change around a lot. From my vantage point, the change is constant and ongoing. That's why what I see on your little blue ball isn't as alarming to me as it is to you because the blue ball will continue to exist. It just may not support your lifestyle. And maybe that's a good thing. Maybe you've pushed things a little too far and it's time for a readjustment to put things into better shape to keep the little blue ball going. At least that's how I understand it from here.

It's not a heartless thing to describe it this way. I love everyone I know there. In fact I love everything about this planet more than I ever did when I was on it. That's because I've learned about this "Force" that is this amazingly wonderful feeling that makes me want to love everything I see. I can't help myself. And I love it all the same. I never could do that when I was there! But when you open to this "Force" you simply have to let go of any hatred or anger you've ever felt. And you want to help everyone and everything because you feel this loving energy inside of you that you never knew you could feel.

So, that's what I feel now. And it is amazing and wonderful. But because I love you, I want to help you. Just like this "Force" only wants to love and help you.

So, whatever changes you see happening there are because you need to let this planet keep on going so it can continue to create life and be part of the gorgeous creation. This is no punishment. You've committed no crime. You've just kind of forgotten who you are and what is so magnificent about where you live and how you got to be alive in the first place. So, you have to change all that so you can remember. And that's what you are doing now. **You are learning to remember once again.**

When you leave the planet, you get to know it. And many of you are leaving and coming to where I am. But you'll go back. And when you do, you'll know more than when you left. At least that's how I see it from here.

•• •• ••

Chapter 5

Paul on Sick Children, True Teachers, and the One Important Lesson

From Linda:

Martin and I had a long talk about this project. He was looking for more structure. Paul seems to want to share what he sees from where he is now. The proposed title given to me by Paul is "Paul Newman, telling it like it is from where he is now." Or something to that effect. I think it gets the point across.

I've been having plenty of dialogues with him as he wakes me up with *James Taylor* playing through my head. I finally got the song out and listened to it. Made me cry. I've heard that song so often and loved it every time. But he's singing it to me. And that's a whole new meaning. "Isn't it amazing a man like me can feel this way? Tell me how much longer, (before we get to work). It grows stronger every day. How much longer?"

Before we begin, I must share some of my dialogue with him. — I asked one question that left me with an amazing answer: *Who was the person he admired and respected the most when he was alive?*

Well, it wasn't *Joe McCarthy!* Much to my astonishment he said he admired *Gen. Dwight D. Eisenhower* the most.

Not the president, but Eisenhower when he was general and won the war in Europe.

He said he was still a good man when he was president, but just got manipulated too much by the establishment when he agreed to be president. He said *Eisenhower* was none too happy about losing his power as president, but there was nothing he could do to stop it. Kind of like what *Obama* is going through now.

He said *Eisenhower* was a reincarnation of *George Washington* who was also a good, principled man. I find that fascinating. He said *Washington* was a member of the *Rosicrucian Society,* which had been founded by *St. Germain.* That is why we have the Masonic symbols on our money. The Free Masons were a branch of the *Rosicrucians.* [I added that here.]

He said *St. Germain* is everywhere and in everything. Paul has a lot of respect for his power and his Light. He says we can't go wrong with that connection. We kind of knew that!

He also liked *Franklin D. Roosevelt,* but not as much because he was unprincipled. He thought FDR was not above using any means necessary to stay in power and do what he wanted to do. Paul thinks *Eleanor* was the real enlightened member of that family. They fought over incarcerating the Japanese during World War II according to what Paul has seen since he's crossed over.

Just as my father and other family members have said, once you go to the higher planes **you can see any part of**

history and get the real picture from there. No propaganda attached. So, that is some of the interesting information that I've heard when I've been half asleep.

I guess it's time for Paul to "tell it like it is" once again:

Hello Linda!

Thanks for getting back to me so soon. I guess my talk with Martin was a bit of a help in galvanizing the two of you into action. [Martin was visited by Paul when he tried to rest this afternoon.] You know, you are a team. Just like me and *Joanne*. That's a rare commodity on your planet. Take advantage of that, and it will make you both stronger. You do know that, don't you?

Now I'd like to talk a bit more about what I've seen of suffering on your planet. You know, *Joanne* and I started those *Hole in the Wall* camps for kids who were very sick. She was my real partner in that, but she didn't care if her name was on the project.

It was one of the most profound things we ever did while I was alive. Oh my God, I learned so much from those kids. Here they'd been through the most devastating illnesses at such young ages, and yet they were full of the zest to live, no matter how compromised life had become. I found that amazing. I'd never really suffered much in my life. Yeah, I lost my boy and that just about killed me. But I'd never gone through what these kids had gone through even before they were old enough to understand the half of what life was all about. Not that grownups figure out much more just 'cause they've grown up.

I loved all these kids. I had to. Couldn't help it. I wanted to give them life and good health. But I couldn't do that. I could just give them some fun. And they were grateful for that. They didn't want more than that. Most of 'em had no idea who I was. Their folks had told 'em, but it didn't matter to them. I was just someone who loved them and that's all they wanted. Most of them only wanted that.

What teachers they were for me!

And that's the point. These kids are incredibly enlightened. They really are teachers! They purposely **chose** those lives to help the rest of us. **They** are the wise ones, the very special ones. Once they get over here, they just glow with Light instantly. Hell, they **glow** with Light even before they arrive. Yes, they suffer there.

Some are starving to death now, or are victims of war, or caught in other tragedies, but once they come here, they are consumed in the Light and instantly take on these forms that will dazzle you.

I was a "star" there. They are the real "Stars," both here and there.

They are choosing this way to open your hearts and make you see what is real and what is not real. Learning to open your hearts and feel honest love for everyone and everything is what is real. Everything else is a lot of hooey.

Fame and wealth are nothing and I have seen often enough how it has not brought anyone real happiness.

The only lasting happiness you will find is when you open your hearts and let this powerful Force, this most amazing energy, fill you and help you end your suffering within yourselves so you can give yourself to helping others.

Those kids healed so much in me. They showed me what was real and what was not real. Loving, just loving for the sake of loving and not because you get anything back in return is what can be real for you there.

These kids didn't know if they would live or die. Most of them had gone through enormous amounts of pain, but when they came together, they made friends, laughed, played, and enjoyed themselves in the most amazing ways. They had no idea if they'd ever see each other again. And they didn't care. Just for that time, they were together, and that was all that mattered.

See, that's the other important thing. You don't get to worry about tomorrow when there may not be a tomorrow. You only have that time together to enjoy yourself. Why can't you all live that way? Let go of what might happen next because you really don't know, do you? The old, "You could get hit by a bus" applies here, right? But that's true, isn't it?

So, just live as if enjoying this particular moment is all that matters because that really is all that matters. Just like these kids were teaching their families to love them now, because tomorrow they might be gone. Treat everyone in your world that way.

Tomorrow will take care of itself. Today you have this time

to open your heart and just love for the sake of loving. And love everything you see. That's how they do it here. Any other feeling just doesn't work once you get here.

I know Linda talked politics with me. We both have that passion in common. But now I don't hate *Joe McCarthy,* and I used to. But I can't do that anymore. I have to love everyone, even him. And it was easy, 'cause now I see him, and his pal *J. Edgar Hoover,* for who they are.

They put on costumes when they got to earth too and were in a truly fascinating drama. But when they got here, where it's real, they had to let go of their costumes and tune into this powerful Force too. And they did. Drama over. Lessons learned.

It happens to everyone eventually. This Force is compelling. As Linda and Martin have heard often, "The Light always wins." And it does. That's something you need to learn to trust there.

I didn't even know about the Light or that it was something I could trust. But I found that energy in the kids and it healed my heart. You don't need to start a camp for sick kids to do this, you know. You can begin now, where you are with the life you're living now.

This is the life you wanted. You may not want to believe that, but it's true. You made that life because that is where you could learn the most. And the most important thing you need to learn is to open your hearts and heal yourselves. I know Karampal wants to talk about that. It's his turn now.

Ask Martin if I'm doing better....

•• •• ••

Chapter 6

Trust the Light, Let Go of Your Fears!

Finally we get a chance to hear from K.P.!

Dearest Linda,

I know it appears that Paul is taking care of most of this message thus far, but he and I are in communication constantly, you know that is possible here, and in these communications we are well aligned in the purpose of this message to you and to all those who care to read what you are writing.

The challenge thus far, as we perceive it, is your concern that others might not believe or care to know what we are sharing with you. But please be aware that we have our finger on the pulse, so to speak, of all humanity at this time, and there is a crying out for more information that will aid them in alleviating the suffering that humanity is experiencing at this time.

You are aware that this time has been foretold. And many are giving this transformation of your planet many different names. Our message to you is to allow you to know that you and all who are living on this planet **have a choice** as to how this will all unfold.

What Paul has shared with you thus far is the key to how

events will unfold. The more that humanity can become aware of how they are experiencing the Light of Infinite Source, the more opportunities each and every one will have in co-creating a truly transcendent outcome for all of this beautiful creation that you call Mother Earth.

I know you were inspired to watch a video of our beautiful homeland, India which was the birth place of much of the philosophical elements that were given to the peoples of the world many centuries ago. This philosophical underpinning was designed to ease humanity into understanding the illusion of duality that exists on Mother Earth. And to leave the confusion of this duality and move to the concept of oneness. To understand that **all of Creation comes from the same source** and allow this source to embrace you as you reside on Mother Earth. To allow this healing, loving radiance to fill you completely and become open, awakened, and aware of the power that will come to you as you open to this Infinite Bliss while you are still embodied.

You, Martin, and I had these moments of Infinite Bliss as we meditated together in India. You know how this can be done. It is very simple, really. It is just the human confusion that makes such a process seem elusive. Even though I had the capability to do this on my own, I often forsook this path to pursue worldly goals and as a result, I suffered.

Now, I am no longer suffering, but am in a place where I can see that if I had stayed on my path to awakening, I need never have suffered in my earthly existence. And this is true for each human.

Events may unfold that seem terrifying. But you need not be terrified if you are completely immersed in your Light and allow it to carry you through the moment. And, of course, it would be incumbent upon you to **trust this Light** as well.

I know you understand completely whereof I speak and yet I know full well you are still confused because each day worry and fear come to you, and you must sit in stillness and call upon the Light once again to help you keep your heart open and full of this loving Light. I know this because each day I am with you observing and aiding you as best I can from this vantage point. More than this, I cannot do.

We are thrilled here that you are taking the time and effort to write down our words. We are with all of you there, lending our support in every way possible to aid you in this opening and awakening. But you must do your part there in order to make this process effective.

First and foremost, you must **let go of your fears regarding the future.** You can't possibly understand yet all that will be happening because you have no frame of reference for what is possible for your planet now. You are entering a force field of higher-vibrational Light that is new to Mother Earth. It will change everything there.

You and I both remember our time in *Durbar Square in Kathmandu* when I asked you, what was the greatest problem on Mother Earth? What was creating all the suffering we observed in the world? And we both knew the answer: **greed.** Fear of lack. That is what killed me. You and I both know this.

And now I see if I had just trusted more that this Light of Infinite Source would always care for me, then I would never had to have the suffering I endured.

I gave in. I allowed it to happen. Do you want that same path, too? I think not. I know that is not true for you. I know you understand that if you give yourself completely to this loving Light, then it will be able to give itself completely to you, and you will be cared for. You, and all you love have nothing to fear except what you choose to fear.

And truly, Linda, what is left to fear? This Light is all-encompassing. It created the magnificent planet upon which you reside. It created the magnificent universe that you see around you. Why would it want any part of this creation to be destroyed? Why would it want any of it to suffer?

First, it's important to understand that it **cannot** be destroyed. What exists is eternal. Absolutely. That is why Paul cannot see where it began — because it has always existed. We have no time. You count time. That is an illusion also. We are here forever.

What we can do is **change form.** And that is what Mother Earth is doing now. She is cleansing and healing herself. And she will succeed in doing this. She will not be destroyed, but she will change form. And this is true for everything upon Mother Earth as well.

So, when you sit in silence and open to this Light of

Infinite Source, you allow yourself to be at the forefront of this transformation process. You are the beginning, the end, and the middle. You are immersed in the greatest reality of all — the reality of Eternal Life in the bosom of Infinite Love from Infinite Source.

You can do that now in this moment and in every moment. You can do that now. Come, I will help you. We will help you. Allow us to help you.

·· ·· ··

Chapter 7

Meditation and an Attitude of Gratitude

From Paul:

I'm beginning to see that Karampal is sure an intelligent guy. His Light shines so brightly here. He says that you, Martin, and he come from one spark of Light. Well, if that is just one third, I can imagine that when the three of you connect up, that's some amazing energy! He says that you did meditate together even when he was alive and you were separated by continents and that this was always a good time for the three of you. I understand that space and time dissolve when you go to that meditation place. It's dissolved here all the time. So meditating across big distances was and is no big deal. That's why we can connect up with you from here.

Karampal, of course, is big on meditation. My meditations were either with a beer bottle or behind the wheel of a very fast vehicle. Usually not at the same time! I really did think of speed racing as a form of getting into the zone, or what you call meditating. I know others who used athletics to get there. These all could have been forms of addiction.

Certainly, beer occupied a big part of my life for a long time. I liked cigarettes, too. Used all that stuff as a way to feel good. But it was never lasting. I think cigarettes helped take me out in the end.

Karampal says he used meditation as his major way to feel good, but that he didn't have the discipline to use it when he most needed it.

See, that's what he wants to make sure people understand now. I can't speak about meditation because I never did it. I mean I tried a couple of times when everyone said how great it was. But I never really understood that you had to do it a lot to feel what was good about it. I didn't have the patience for that.

I had lots of good feelings in my life, like when I was at the *Hole in the Wall* camps, so I wasn't actually seeking to find more ways to feel good. — I guess there's different ways to get there.

But now that I'm here and I feel how powerful this Force is and know that this is what folks find when they do meditate, I understand what Karampal is talking about and I can see that I wasted a lot of time trying to find this Force in other things. I mean I know this Force is in everything, but I would have liked to feel that while I was alive. That's the big thing I missed about my life. Knowing about this. I had to get here to find it.

But what Karampal says is that everyone can find this powerful Force now while they are on the planet. That this is getting much easier to do and he wants this understanding to be clear with all of you there. **Finding this Force while you are alive is the key to making the changes happen**

for the whole planet in the best way possible.

What you are seeing on the planet now is a great deal of destruction brought on by the fears and anger of a helluva lot of people there. Everyone seems to be in destruct mode instead of construct mode. Or at least, that's how it looks from here. I know you guys are trying to help, and others like you. But are there enough of you doing this meditating often enough to keep the powerful Light coming in to your planet?

Why are so many still choosing to have a miserable time there? Because you are too afraid to sit still long enough and let yourselves do it all another way? Do you see a mountain of trouble and decide it will be too difficult to make that mountain dissolve, so instead you give up and brace yourself for the hurricane, tornado, war, earthquake, or general calamity that you assume must happen? But **it doesn't have to be this way.**

See, that's the whole point. **You don't have to go through this hell.** And that's where hell is, you know. It's not here. It's there. You make it happen there. Here, there is just a lot of love and help. You're just all agreeing that that is all there is to life, so that is all there is to it.

Go fix lunch, Linda. I'll wait......

You know, for the most part, Linda and Martin have figured out something there. They know there is more than one way to meditate. Karampal says this is true. It isn't just when you are still that you can open to let in this powerful energy. It can happen when you are moving around too. It's called **appreciating all that is wonderful in your life now.**

I can see through everything now. I never could do that there. Not just the skin on the surface, but right through your whole body. And I see the energy, the Light flowing through everything there. It's magnificent. It's gorgeous. This Light has so many glorious colors to it. It's really indescribable. But I try anyway. Used to using words. No words for this, though. So, you have all this Light coursing through you in every moment, making your heart beat, keeping you going. *Do you ever feel gratitude for that?*

Do you ever look at the gorgeous planet you live on? The place is teeming with life and all this life is filled with the same Light that is keeping you going. That's the Force I'm talking about. Everything has it. I just got to understand it once I got here. While I was there, I had absolutely no idea about any of this. I just thought what you see is what you get. But now I see that I was actually blind. Not seeing anything that was real. This energy flowing through you and everything there is what is real.

When you cut open an apple and taste it, you can make that one of your meditations. Think of the apple as this powerful force of energy that you are taking into your amazing body that is filled with the same Force. Say, "Thanks, this is great!" See, I think that's a meditation. Can you spend your whole day doing that?

That would be an amazing start to turning your whole

world around. Can you get out of yourself and your own gloom and doom enough to see how great the planet is now? Can you build on that apple and take it into everything that is amazing and wonderful about the place you chose to live?

It wasn't a bad choice, really. Yes, there are places like it all through the universe. You guys can't see that there. It's part of the blindness. But if you could open your eyes and really, really see, what you would find would seem utterly amazing and glorious to you.

Start by assuming that you can see. Act. Pretend. You can do that. **Just start saying thank you whether you understand it or not.** Your world is really beautiful. From here, we can see what is wonderful. The trees, the flowers, the sky, the Earth. It's all glorious. The more of you who open your eyes to know this powerful Force within everything the more you will create that this is all you can and will see. You make that happen.

Linda and Martin have found a beautiful place to live in this world. They have created a heaven on Earth for themselves. They have allowed themselves to learn to say "thank you" often enough that it has transformed their lives. You can do the same. Yes, do that meditating, too. I see how important that is now. Karampal can explain more about that. But what I am telling you about is **how to make every moment count.** I hear from everyone here that this is important too.

·· ·· ··

40

Chapter 8

Awakening the Kundalini Energy

From Linda:

It's been a couple of weeks since I've had time to write more for this book. My sister came for a visit from the U.S. and the children were on summer break from school. I had to let go of any quiet time to work on the book to be with the family instead. It was an enjoyable time, especially having my sister here for her first visit. But now that the children are back in school, it's time to fulfill other agreements I have made. And writing this book is one of them.

I re-read the last chapter to get a sense again of what Paul and K.P. are endeavoring to do here. Paul is so honest and clear to me. It is another perspective from someone who was so recently living in the Western world where meditation and mysticism have only recently gained wider acceptance. This is the world that I grew up in as well.

K.P. died around the same time Paul transitioned. But he was in India in his last lifetime, an Eastern and Asian environment. He was exposed to the most powerful force fields possible on the Earth plane that are conducive to creating a meditative state. This made it much easier for him to embrace and accept the precepts that they are sharing with us now.

The contrast between these two men in their last lifetimes is what I'm finding fascinating to observe. Now they are in a place where they can find a common meeting ground that would never have been possible while they were alive. They appear to have great respect for each other as well.

Given our current political climate in the U.S., I can easily compare this to a staunch Republican and the most liberal Democrat dying and going to heaven. Once they pass through the "Pearly Gates" they realize that all that stuff they were fighting about on Earth was really rather ridiculous.

The reality is that we are all from the same Source and any differences are illusions. Ah! If only everyone in the world could figure that out now!

From Karampal:

Dearest Linda,

It is so good to be connecting with you once again in this manner. Although you have certainly been aware that Paul and I have not left your side for one moment while you have been occupied with other matters.

I am especially appreciative that you and *Namita* [K.P.'s daughter] have remained in contact and that she is more actively seeking your help at this time.

You do know that this is also the work that you and Martin have agreed to do. As well as opening more fully to your own Light, you will be helping many more open to their Light as well. In this sense, your work will never end, just as our work is not ending although we are no longer in physical form on your planet.

Changing form only changes one thing. You no longer have a body. But you don't lose any of your consciousness. That is why when people take their own lives, they realize very quickly that they haven't lost any of the discomforts that caused them to make this decision. They still must do the healing that is necessary for them to move into the Light.

I know it becomes easy to judge others who appear confused because of their ignorance of the true nature of reality. But rest assured, there is a portion of every entity, human or otherwise, that continues to reside in the Light of Infinite Source. This Light is constantly feeding everyone there and offering them a line of energy to move out of their confusion and more fully into their Light.

The miraculous part of this is that **you do not have to wait until you die to have this experience.** And that is what I have come to tell you about now.

Yes, as Paul has said, I have been actively connecting with my Light for many years. Now that I have lost the distraction of a physical form, this is much simpler to do. I can see and know the reality that I was pursuing while I was alive on your planet.

I will tell you now that what we learned from the ancient mystics about the true nature of reality was accurately portrayed. **There is a fountain of information available in many of the ancient texts,** some of which we helped write many centuries ago. Now you are recording these truths again in a modern language so that these generations can know what we originally wrote in Sanskrit.

The truth remains the same. It is constant.

As you breathe deeply into your naval region, you will feel a conscious awareness of this powerful Light that is flowing through you in every moment. You can then open each chakra region, beginning with the root chakra that resides at the tip of the spine. Your goal is to get the serpent power to rise through your spinal column. This is the *kundalini* energy that is already within you. Once it is activated fully within your form, you carry a power that is unequaled by anything man can create simply by building muscle.

This energy is what is tapped in all the forms of Martial Arts that have manifested on your planet. It is not through physical power that you accomplish the amazing feats that these masters have achieved. Absolutely not. It is through tapping the mystical powers known through the centuries that man attains his greatest strength. This is the power that I want you to know more fully. This is what I am here to teach you now. Complete physical transformation is possible with this power. You can know and activate what I activated but did not use properly when I was alive. Thus, the *kundalini* energy subverted in me and wasted my form.

Learn what we know here and this will never happen to you or Martin.

You are at the gate. Now walk through the door.

•• •• ••

Chapter 9

Paul on Activism of a Different Kind

From Linda:

After the last chapter so many events unfolded in our lives that it has taken me two months to return to writing this book. This has not stopped Paul and K.P. from communicating with me on the higher planes. It has simply stopped me from writing what I have continued to receive.

What finally pushed me to make time to write, were two lovely e-mails that arrived:

Hi Linda:

We are very grateful for all the beautiful messages and lessons you share with all. I wonder if you can tell me if there is more communication with Paul Newman? It was very interesting to find his communication. Thanks a lot for sharing.

Blessings and love from the heart, Miryam

Upon my response, Miryam wrote:

Yes, perhaps you are right about Paul for he comes to my mind often, specially this past two weeks. It seemed to me that he is in such urgency as to almost shout this truth that he has found. "Dear one, your book will be a great success. Don't take too long for we have not much time."

[...]

Namaste, Miryam

Miryam's emails were telling me words that I was also hearing within, and now I knew I had to get back to the book!

Martin and I have heard repeatedly that we had lifetimes as Rishis, i.e., scribes that had shared the messages from the higher planes with those who followed the Hindu religion.

This, of course, was many centuries ago, but those words of wisdom still hold great value today. I appreciate that I had chosen that path — but wondered what more I could offer now?

It apparently doesn't matter what I think about all this with my ego mind. What seems to be most important is that I continue to share these messages.

Now it is Paul's turn to offer his words of wisdom. With all the political upheaval on the Earth plane, particularly the "Occupy" movement [in 2011], and Paul's interest in politics, he most definitely has something to say!

From Paul:

Well, thanks, Linda for giving me a platform here. I know

you have been busy. You've told me that more than once when I've come to you. That's okay. I understand that. I remember that I was always so busy that I didn't have time to open myself up to any of this "stuff."

At least you kept up your communication with the Light, and once in awhile when you asked for help, I was there too. You know that. You have a great deal of love and respect here from the folks you call "beings of Light." It appears that there is no limit to what they'd do to help you from the higher planes, as you call it. Although, right now at this moment, I'm sitting right next to you. There is really no "up there" as you conceive it. We are just on another dimension, or frequency. That's why all those guys who study quantum physics are finally figuring something out there that could be pretty important and significant for everyone to understand, if they put their mind to it, which I'm guessing most people won't.

Right now, everyone seems caught up in counting numbers. Who has too much? Who has too little? Who has enough? Not too many folks think they have enough, and **everybody** is worried about the future! That's for sure!

Are you? Sometimes, we see you vacillating between trusting and worrying. But mostly you seem to be trusting. This whole trusting business is a real problem there, isn't it? What's real? What's not?

Well, I'll tell you what's real. What is coming through you now from me. **I am more "real" now than I ever was when I was alive.** Then, I was just a figment of my

47

imagination, acting out a script everyday to satisfy a bunch of ego needs. But nothing I was doing ever actually completely satisfied me. This drove *Joanne* crazy.

She'd done something that was completely satisfying to her. She'd had kids. I mean, they were my kids too, but I hadn't made them. Hadn't contributed all that much to them. That was her job, and it was a good one.

But all the creative stuff I'd done was one way of flirting with all of myself, but never completely taking it all in so that I could feel really good about me and who I was. That was because *I didn't actually know who I was.*

Now I do. You've touched that knowledge, but it's not completely in you either. That is the process you call "awakening." And you only seem to completely wake up once you die. I mean, some folks do it while they are alive, but not too many.

We know you've flirted with dying more than once. My son flirted with it, and he did die. Now he's here, and we've had some good talks about the difference of life as you know it and how "alive" we feel here. There is such a difference! But I'm not advocating that you take your life so you can find out.

What I'm advocating is that you take the time to find out as much as you can about life in all its forms. Here and there, which is actually here, just on another level. You're not even a stone's throw away. **You are right here! I am right here!**

So what's the confusion all about that everyone is going through there? Why are you rocking this beautiful blue ball in ever crazier ways? What is so unfair? Why are you all continuing to fight so much with one another?

What difference does it make how much money everyone has? Why do you need more? Why does someone else have less? What don't you have? What have you lost? What must you have?

There are places on your planet where the people are dying because they are starving. Once they come here, they are filled again and finally find peace in their souls and spirits. What's filled them up? The same thing that could fill up all the angry people there.

Only no one wants to stop being angry long enough to find out what that is.

And boy, is everyone angry. **When you get that angry, you close off.** When you close off, you miss the whole message of why you are there. Bitter and angry. Everyone is getting bitter and angry. Is that starving baby bitter and angry or just hungry? How about the mother who will hold a dead child in her arms?

Is anyone thinking about these folks?

We are. We are very busy with these folks, helping them to fill with the Light once they come to this frequency. This is all happening in the same space you are in. They are not far away. That's some confusion you have there.

It's all happening on top of itself. I know that's so hard for you to understand.

I know your main mission that you agreed to was to just write and share your writing. And you are doing a damn good job of that. You are. But learn something from what you are writing. Learn to give your big bright Light away more fully to everyone and everything that needs it there. Ask for this Light to flood your planet. Be that beacon there. Put it into words, but *let the Light be a beacon of action too.*

You've given a lot of yourself to your children, and that's great. But you have a lot more to give to the world.

So many **people need to "get over" themselves** and see that the picture is a lot bigger. A lot bigger. Think about how you can help your planet and everyone and everything on it. Start by filling yourself with this Light and giving it to the planet. Just radiate it.

That's a good girl. Then ask to be shown what else you can do to support this change that is happening to your planet now. You are there, and we are here. Be a link to make that support happen. **Ask us to do more.**

Don't limit yourselves. **Spread yourselves out.** Let this Light flow through you in every direction.

Do you want to stop being angry and find this peace you all talk about? I was really big on peace when I was there. Talked about it a lot. A whole lot. But I was angry that we didn't have peace. Crazy, huh?

Lots of people are still that crazy. Can't be angry. Can't be "against" war and think that's a way to end it.

See, all those old ideas are dying now. They have to.

The only thing that's gotten people out of their chairs and into the streets is that they aren't as comfortable as they were. As long as the Earth was taking the "hit" for all that comfort they were enjoying, they'd stay in their chairs. But once the comforts started disappearing, they hit the streets.

But what about the planet and the people who've never had anything taken away from them, because they never had anything in the first place? Aren't all of the folks who are complaining in the 10% who've been happily exploiting the planet to be so comfortable?

Time to take action, Linda. But a different sort. Tell the truth. Tell it like it is. Don't think you must have it all in order to be happy if "all" means more, more, more.

We have none of that stuff here. We have something else that is worth a lot more.

We know who we are now.

•• •• ••

Chapter 10

Kundalini and the Paths to Awakening

From Linda:

Now I know it's time to hear from K.P., but after his message on kundalini and its repercussions through our systems I am a bit worried that he might open up more energy centers that may need further purging. Because he is our Twin Flame, he carries a great deal of power in creating these "cleansing" processes in us. I haven't ever been appreciative of this, although the Light does grow stronger within me afterwards.

My question is the same as the one I hear from many we work with:

Isn't there an easier way?

From Karampal (who refers to us here by our spirit names Leia and Manalus):

Dearest Leia,

Although we remain in constant communication, I do appreciate the opportunity to contribute to this book, and help all those who seek our support in their awakening process.

Last time, you did allow a further opening of your kundalini energy after some clearing and healing, and this has led to an increased power in the Light you and Manalus now carry.

It has been easily noticeable to us here to observe this. And you have both felt the change in your systems as well.

But your question remains, *Is there an easier way to open and clear your chakra system so the Light might flow through with less difficulty?*

You do know the answer to this as well as I do. If you were to acknowledge each moment of emotional discomfort as an opportunity to clear and heal a chakra region, then there would be no necessity of feeling the physical discomfort that plagued you recently.

You know that **physical discomfort always follows emotional discomfort.** This is one of the main tenets of the work that you and Manalus offer in helping others to heal themselves.

This is what you offered to me as healing prior to my departure from the Earth plane.

For me, the issue centered in my heart chakra. I was experiencing great emotional pain there that translated into the physical illness that ended my life.

What were the emotions that ultimately did clear in the *kundalini* region as you went through your physical difficulties?

You see, the *kundalini* region at the tip of the spine

not only directly relates to one's sexuality, but also to one's relationship to having a physical form and walking on your beautiful planet.

The adrenals are easily affected when this region is compromised, because a rush of adrenaline will fill your form in response to any experience of fear.

Humans frequently have fears for their safety, so this region is often affected.

What were your fears that were in need of addressing as you opened the *kundalini* once again?

Part of the issue for you is the decline in sexuality as you add more years to your life.

This has been very difficult for you to address because so much of a human's identity is related to being sexually active. And yet, you have realized that as you've opened even further to your Light, the need for this identification has lessened. Your fear then, was in losing Manalus if you were not sexually active with him. This was very frightening to you, based on past life karma and your current situation.

A basic fear of survival became quite relevant — and the physical pain and suffering began.

As you healed your physical pain, and the *kundalini* was able to open more fully, you realized that the Light that was flowing through ever more powerfully could and would carry you through any circumstances that might arise.

Your love for Manalus also strengthened as you spoke of

your worries and fears with him and you both realized that perhaps strengthening the Light within was an even more powerful bond that you both have than expressing your love in a sexual manner.

Your training in the power of the *kundalini* has shown you that when you take this energy in all its forms, including sexual, and allow it to rise through your spine, it strengthens your whole system and brings you to greater alignment with your Light.

And this is the path that you and Manalus have now chosen.

It is a sacred path and one that frees you to use all your energy toward healing and transforming your forms to be of greatest service to the Light in every way.

Of course, if one chooses to remain sexual, this does not detract from one's ability to open and awaken. But opening and clearing one's *kundalini* will increase the rapidity and strengthening of the awakening.

All are sovereign beings of Light upon your plane, and all will have the freedom to choose whatever process can lead to this awakening. Some will simply choose to transition, as Paul and I have done.

Others will choose to activate the *kundalini* to move the process along. This is what you and Manalus have chosen. And others will choose to allow a gradual chakra cleansing and healing. This is viable as well. No one path is perfect for everyone, but everyone's path is perfect for each one.

Allow this process of opening and clearing to continue now. This strengthens your ability to be of greater service to the Light. And that is why you are all in physical form at this time.

You know we continue to support you in this process in every way possible.

It is an exciting time to be alive!

•• •• ••

Chapter 11

The Power of Thoughts – Here and There

From Linda:

It's encouraging to read the response from a few readers who've looked at these recent chapters. K.P.'s voice is so different from Paul's and yet no one doubts the veracity of what they are sharing.

Because these two beings of Light are with me frequently now, even when I'm not directly open to channeling for the book, I'm feeling more and more comfortable about continuing to write this. Their presence has helped me feel an urgency to get the book completed and sent out to a wider audience.

From Paul:

Hello Linda!

It's good to see you making progress on the writing. Nice to know Martin approves of you "hanging out" with me. He's not a jealous fellow. That's a rarity in any world. Oh yeah, there are folks who get jealous here. We aren't on the same plane as those Ascended Master types, at least not yet. More learning for me to do here first. But I've been given the "go ahead" to work with you because so many people feel comfortable knowing that there are steps that can be taken when you cross over to this side and that you aren't expected to know it all right away before you move on to those higher planes.

Oh, we all interact with one another frequently from the different planes, and as your father and Martin's father have told you, we can "skate the ethers," (the energy fields) and go into other times and spaces to view them from this perspective.

One of the interesting things I've noticed, (there are so many) is that all I have to do is think about something, and bam! It's happening. That's really helped me to watch what I'm thinking. It's also helped me realize how powerful my thoughts were when I was alive.

How often I actually planned my life's path without realizing it. I mean, I actually planned my life's path *all the time.* Which is still something I'm not always comfortable dealing with as I review my life here. We get plenty of time to review our lives. It's part of the program. And when we've healed all the stuff we feel about our lives, then we move on to another level where the Light really fills us up in a completely new way.

I'm looking forward to that. But I'm not quite there yet. One reason I have stuck around at this level is to write all this up with you because that is an important part of my "karmic" growth. Which, I guess, leads you to a big question you've been wanting an answer to.

In addition to living in the same neighborhood, and being part of the same "tribe" (religion), how did we know each other before so that we'd have such a big connection now?

Well, that's actually a long story and it didn't begin on the Earth. We were all part of a group that chose to come to the Earth a long, long time ago when it was decided that we'd be what you now call human forms. We pre-dated the dense physical bodies you all have there now.

Our bodies were pretty light and airy, as I've seen them when I've had this thought and been taken to that time. We moved about kind of the same way I do now. Just traveled by thinking about where we wanted to be and what we wanted to do. You call the place we come from Arcturus. But it's a bit more complicated than that and a little beyond what you can understand there. Arcturus is a good enough term to help you relate. Eventually, you'll understand more about that. But just take it in steps the way I do here for now.

In fact, from what I understand, anyone who reads this will have come from the same place.

We've all remained connected by thoughts that are beyond your idea of thinking throughout the life spans of humans on Earth. At times, we've been together as humans, at other times some have been on the higher planes and interacted with those on Earth.

In fact, before you were born, while I was already on Earth, we were connecting.

It doesn't make a lot of sense, since everything seems very linear and "one on one" there, but it looks possible from here.

You've had that vision of the hologram with everything sandwiched together on top of itself, and therefore easy to connect to different times and spaces. That's a good way to look at it. And then you had that vision of a part of the hologram splitting off and entering your time and space there at an angle to penetrate your frequency. That is correct too. I come into your conscious awareness on such an angle.

Fascinating to watch from here because **I can slice into your planet anywhere at any time all the time and stay equally connected.** Whenever anyone thinks of me there, I pick up the signal and show up energetically to see what's coming down. I don't always like what I see, which is why I'm grateful to be able to set some of this straight by talking with you in this way.

Once you cross over and go to the funeral or whatever of those coming to either celebrate your life, mourn your loss, or celebrate your death, you'll be amazed how **you can "read" everyone's mind** and understand what they are all thinking, all at the same time!

I'll tell you, in the beginning, that wasn't very pleasant, and I needed a lot of help from folks who'd been through that here to get my bearings and not explode! Some of the bull crap that folks were saying was just terrible. I knew a lot of that stuff when I was alive, but it wasn't all coming at me at the same time, and I could turn a lot of it off. Couldn't do that here. Had to learn to open up and let this Light carry me through this. It isn't all angels coming to greet you, and I didn't see a bunch of virgins either. Looked for those.

It was just a lot of energy rushing at me, and feeling incredibly loved like I'd never felt that love on Earth. And then your group showed up around you, and I knew I was in good territory.

Never understood the word **"compassion"** on Earth. It's big here as a concept. Had to learn to use compassion when connecting to all the bull crap I was hearing and seeing there. All that confusion comes from people suffering with closed hearts. When you completely open your heart, you can't be that mean and awful any more. It's impossible. That's why it's a good idea to get into that part of the program while you are there, so when you come here, it doesn't hit you so hard all at once. Besides, it makes life easier there too. Then you begin to understand that it really doesn't matter what anyone else is thinking or saying about you, because you've got all that love in your heart from the one source that matters, and that's really all that matters.

I know you understand this. I know you do. I see you doing this all the time. You won't let yourself stay miserable about anything because you want that connection to this amazing Light to fill your heart.

That's worth more than anything you can have on the Earth. You've taken great strides to know that. Important information. I mean I can keep telling you how it is here. And that's important to know too. Some of it you just can't understand yet, and I probably won't be able to explain. You know you already spend a great deal of time here and on the higher planes when you meditate and definitely when you sleep. A lot of that can't even be memories for you because memories need words. So, you see how limited I am in what I can tell you.

Hey! I'll tell you what! Some time when you are meditating, ask me or Karampal or some other high-power dude to show you more. Oh, you've done that already. Well, ask again. There's more to see, and it really is fantastic.

Ah, I see your cat is ready for dinner. You know she's one of us, too, and has been with you forever? She's amazing, isn't she? So many of our animal friends are. Don't discount their intelligence. They are just as perceptive as we are, just without all the verbal "hogwash" that humans enjoy.

•• •• ••

Chapter 12

Allow Your Identity to Fall Away

From Linda:

After the message from Paul yesterday, I decided to try his idea. During my early morning meditation I asked for help from the beings of Light, particularly *Archangel Michael,* to open myself more fully to an awareness of the higher planes.

Instead of a deep meditation, I fell into a dream state. I was in a park of some sort where masses of people were being entertained by a group of singers in costume. I found myself in some sort of lawn chair, sitting next to a lovely elderly woman who wanted to know about my life. I said I was married to Martin, who appeared nearby and that I had many children, one of whom was sitting in my lap. He was a beautiful, blond-haired boy of about three or four years.

She asked me his name and to my consternation, I didn't know his name. I felt he was a child of mine, but I couldn't remember what I called him. The boy leapt from my lap, and ran to join Martin who was leaving the park. I called after them, but Martin said I could find my own way, and he wasn't going to stay with me. Neither was the boy. I thought that maybe Martin would have his cell phone, so I tried to remember that number, but the only number in my head was my social security number, which I began reciting over and over as a way to remember who I was. This woke me from my dream.

I asked what that was about, and heard that if I was going to move to the higher planes, I'd have to *give up my identity* as a wife and mother. I devote a great deal of my day caring for my family, worrying about them and trying to be as effective and nurturing as possible as a parent. What I was being told was to let go of all this effort to be this person, and instead allow my Light to enfold me more fully and carry me through to an easier and more effective way to be available to all, not just those I identify with as my mate and my children.

I was still feeling the discomfort from the dream, so I tried meditating again, and this time a huge, massive light did engulf me to such an extent that I came out of the meditation quickly before I was completely consumed by it.

Not the most auspicious beginning for me as I move to the greater awakening that we are hearing about here!

And now it's Karampal's turn once again.

Hello Leia,

I understand that you are still experiencing some difficulty in allowing a complete enfoldment in your Light. I remember these challenges well! I never really released myself fully because I also had taken the path of a family person who felt my responsibilities deeply.

I only wished all in my family to be well and happy but found, much to my consternation, that I was not able to give them either health or happiness. They would all need to find that for themselves.

Unfortunately, by the time I realized this, I had completely lost my health trying to care for them and ultimately I lost my life. It is a tale I've told more than once, but it is a cautionary message for you and Manalus, is it not?

Now, you and Manalus are being given this opportunity to open to your Light and to grow ever more rapidly. More rapidly than it was possible for me. It is easier for you now because the frequencies have increased for everyone to embrace.

But are you trying to follow the same path as I did? Or will you allow your identity as you've known yourself to this time to fall away, so you can become who you truly are while still in human form?

We understand your worries and fears about letting go. It is frightening. It was too frightening for me, so I didn't do it, even though this is what I yearned for my whole life.

Just as I worried about my family's well being, you worry also. How can they get by without you interacting at the level they expect of you? And even more important for me was what society would think of me if I was not caring for my family as was expected of me.

My wife made it very plain that this would be unacceptable. Very unacceptable. So, I acceded to these demands and lost the chance to open completely while I was alive.

But is this your and Manalus' journey as well? And what

about those who are reading this book? Are they reading this book so they can remain static in their lives and not open as fully as possible at this time of great awakening for all of humanity?

I understand my path was perfect for me so that I could move to the higher planes and be of service from this perspective. This is true for Paul as well. But this is not true for you, Manalus, and those who are reading these words.

Your path is different than ours. You are choosing awakening while in human form and yes, this does entail letting go of your identity as you've known yourself to this time.

Now, there is much about your identity that has gratified your ego. Isn't that true? You've enjoyed being known as a good wife and mother. Capable and efficient. Able to master many tasks and do them well. Successful, intelligent, interesting, entertaining, and yes, quite attractive to many.

Lovely attributes, but not necessary to opening to one's Light. There is only one attribute that is actually necessary. And that would *be to surrender all ego-driven perceptions of self* in favor of one perception: that **you are a vehicle of Light** and you will completely embrace this Light and let it be who you are as you walk upon your planet.

Much to your surprise, you will notice all worry, fear, and challenges of any sort to dissolve as you allow yourself to embrace this Light completely.

And, just as you have shared with many, many others, you can now know for yourself that opening ever more fully to your Light **does not take you away from life,** but allows you to live life in an effortless grace.

This is why your worries and fears dissolve. You have no need any longer to worry or fear about anything. You know the Light will carry you through everything. You know this and allow this. There is no ego to stop you from this opening, trusting, and allowing.

Now, what are the challenges to allowing this to occur? There seem to be many. First, it is your **conditioning.** Both Manalus and I suffered with a childhood filled with admonitions that if we didn't straighten ourselves out, we would surely fail. It was a competitive world that we had entered, and only the best, brightest, and most driven would succeed. This message did not resonate with either of us. We are dreamers and visionaries. This race to success was anathema to our souls and spirits. We were sure there was a better way, we just didn't know what that could be. Although I lived in a land that showed me this path more easily, my conditioning continually led me to believe that such a path would be foolhardy to follow. Such was the case for Manalus. "Be practical" became the motto we were to live by.

We rebelled as best we could, only to be chastised continuously for our foolhardy behavior. Twin Flames in spirit, continents apart, but still living the same story. Is this not true, beloved friend?

As for Leia, she was taught early on to live by her wits and be a survivor. She succeeded in feeding her children and caring for many. She is the possessor of a magnanimous spirit who prides herself in giving and caring. But at what cost to her soul and spirit? It is commendable to care for others, most certainly. But it is also gratifying to receive praise for our efforts. Opening to one's Light completely and losing one's identity might lead to others believing that Leia had forgotten how to be giving and loving. That was anathema to her.

Yes, **you are simultaneously being asked to forget who you are as an ego construct, and remember who you are in reality.** When you are embraced by your Light, then you will be more easily able to embrace others without losing your true identity. Being a success or failure becomes irrelevant because you have embraced what is relevant, which is your true Self. *You are Light.*

This Light cares for all of your beautiful creation, beloved friends. When you allow it to embrace you fully and completely it will care for you as well.

Can you do this? Can you trust this? Can you let go and completely be your Light now?

Ask for our help and we can show you the way.

•• •• ••

Chapter 13

There is Only One Rule: Let the Light Love You Unconditionally

From Linda:

Well, yesterday turned out to be pretty interesting for Martin and for me. After a few days of "lectures" here from Paul and K.P. and some pretty intense channeling sessions from *Lahiri Mahasaya,* the guru who initiated *Yogananda's* parents as well as his guru *Sri Yukteswar,* our lives began to change very noticeably.

During the channeling session as *Lahiri Mahasaya* reiterated what we'd been receiving for this book, Martin and I became aware that Martin's plan to have blood tests to decipher what foods would work best in his system might be unnecessary. We were being guided to trust this Light to tell us all that we would need to know. By giving our power away and seeking costly tests to determine what Martin needed, we were once again disallowing what we'd learned and who we are. Information began to flow to me about what foods would be best for Martin, and I shared what I was receiving. Martin researched the information and decided to give this new system a try. He then received a registration for a meditation class that he had planned to begin that evening. The class was held, and he received money for the class that he was then able to use directly to purchase the food today that will increase his health and well being. During our channeling this morning, we were offered the understanding of how Martin had allowed the Light to quite tangibly take care of his needs.

Yesterday, I was a bit depressed because I was unable to shake this feeling of loss that was coming to me as I contemplated letting go of my ego identity as a mother even further. During our evening meal both of our children volunteered that their friends think I'm "cool."

They proceeded to discuss this even further with each other, and as I questioned them if this could possibly be true, they assured me that even though I'm very old to be the Mom of two young, adolescent children, their friends did indeed find me to be "cool."

Wow! That was amazing. So, by walking away from my "need" to be a good Mom and giving away to my "need" to be engulfed by my Light may not be such a bad plan after all. I had to laugh at myself over this.

I'm sure Paul will find this all pretty funny too.

From Paul:

No, Linda, I don't find it funny or even humorous. Well, okay, it's kind of humorous. But what I do think is great is how open you both are becoming as we bombard you with this information.

Karampal and I were like racehorses, at the starting gate, just waiting for you to open the gate and let us in. You knew we were there, but chose to let everything and anything else get in the way until we had to come through another source to get the point across. And now that you are letting this Light in more powerfully, you are wondering why it took you so long to let it all happen.

You see, this is very typical of what you've also seen in the work you do. This ego identification business can be a real drag. I know that for sure. Many times I was given the opportunity to get out of the way and let something bigger and better carry me through a situation but I was determined not to "tarnish" my image of who I was and what I would do.

Some people thought I was pretty smart for how I did that. Others thought I was a real asshole. Now I think of it as me being a smart asshole. But I was convinced that I had all the answers. Absolutely.

That's why getting here has been so humbling for me. I knew jackshit about what was really going down. I really thought I lived in the center of the world. And actually we all do live in the center of the universe in our own world that we create. We create it. But, we create it out of ignorance. Because, see, **this universe is huge.** You have no idea. No idea.

It's just amazing and gorgeous beyond your wildest imagination. You are residing in a miracle and you're messing up how you can live in it because you've kept on the blinders for a very long time now. You're all picking lint out of your belly buttons and bemoaning how life is not the way you'd like it to be.

You are throwing away amazing opportunities to live completely in this gorgeous universe while you are alive. Just **getting out of the way** and letting this Light fill you up is the first step. It really does work.

This universe is so vast, so huge, so perfect that you've just got to believe in God or whatever you want to call it. Whatever has created all this doesn't really care at all what you call it.

This is the amazing part to me. We don't get punished here for being smart assholes while we are alive. We punish ourselves by shortchanging ourselves and living within some stupid set of rules that don't mean a damn thing once you get here.

There is only one rule here. Let this Light love you unconditionally. Let it fill you, and then radiate that out in every direction.

That's it. That's all there is to it. If everyone would take off the blinders there, war would end instantly. Suffering would end. Disease would end. Everyone would have enough of everything because everyone would be willing to share everything with everyone else. The thought of having more than someone else wouldn't even dawn on anyone.

You know, we gave a lot away, *Joanne* and I. But we still had more than enough of everything. Way more than enough. And everyone we knew had more than enough.

Hell, we knew people were suffering in other places. We weren't blind to that. And we shared and we cared. But now I see I wouldn't have even wanted that big house or those fast cars or any of that. But it felt good, you see, to have that stuff.

Now I see I would have felt *even better* if I'd given it all away.

Because you know, once you are here you realize that this was still way too much. None of it comes with you. You know that play, *You Can't Take it With You.* Well, that's the truth! So what was that about anyway? That was one of my rules there, though. I have to make some money when I work. Why? I don't know why.

Some actors make an obscene amount of money. Why? I actually never knew the answer to that. We really have a fun job. It's fun to act. We just don't know that while we are alive we all are acting all the time. And we take it far too seriously. Because we are **afraid of everything**. So, if things don't happen the way we think they should, then we get all mean and ugly and nasty. Can't do that now. Don't even want to. And I regret how many times I did that while I was alive. Looks pretty stupid now. Yet, I can't feel that way.

This compassion thing grabs hold and then I just feel this amazing love in my heart when I look at those times. And when that happens I see the whole thing healing. See, that's what I mean. This God or whatever only wants us to be filled with this love and to send it in every direction, *even into anything bad that we did when we were alive.*

Just heal it all and let this love fill the situation while this love fills us.

And it isn't the love you knew when you were alive where if you said "I love you" you expected someone to say that back to you or you'd get all hurt and angry.

Here, you just feel it inside you and even if no one says "I love you" back, it doesn't matter. **You've got so much love inside you and the supply is never ending.** So you just spread it around. That's all you want to do.

•• •• ••

Chapter 14

Keep Your Heart Open and Ask for Help

From Linda:

Paul's message was beautiful and it should have been helpful. I'm all for opening my heart and letting the Light fill me. I can do that. Some of the time. But then I end up getting very disappointed when the other people in my universe just don't get it.

I do pride myself on being an effective communicator. I really think I know how to get the point across. And I will try to speak from an open, loving heart only to be rebuffed and refuted. Misunderstood. Then, I back up and try again. But now I'm a bit angry and hurt that this open, loving heart is being pounded on by someone with whom I'm trying to communicate. Why does this happen this way? If I'm truly making an effort to be open and loving in every moment, to "give my Light away" as I've been advised so often by the beings of Light, then why does this rebuff occur? And why do I feel so hurt and angry when it happens? My motives are misconstrued. If I really try to clarify myself, then I get rebuffed even more. I'm amazed each time this happens. It makes me very shy and hesitant to try again. What's up with that? All I want to do is back away completely and not even try to connect with those who choose not to hear, feel, or understand me. It's too challenging for me to push on when this happens. I want to give up altogether.

It's Karampal's turn:

Dear, darling Leia, we do understand the confusion you experience. We've all experienced similar situations, many times. I most certainly know what you are saying here. This happened so many times with me that I ultimately gave up even trying to communicate what I knew and understood. The clarity escaped me as the surrounding confusion filled my ears.

And we also see that the situation for many has not improved with time. As the frequencies increase and so many resist this powerful Light, the challenges become more constant for those seeking to open and simply fill their hearts with Light and healing.

You are bombarded daily by those who are not ready to be open and choose not to understand who you are and what you are offering.

How do you remain centered, calm, and filled with Light when you are so continuously surrounded by this confusion? Obviously, you don't and then your physical and emotional wellbeing are compromised. You know we understand here, because we all experienced the same challenges. Everyone who opens to the Light goes through a similar experience.

We have been taught by the Masters through the centuries that **the path to awakening is a rocky one,** filled with opportunities that challenge us to stay open and continue.

Great mystics through the ages have been actively persecuted, as you are well aware, and during these times of persecution were still being asked by the loving Light to allow it to continue to embrace them even in the most perilous of moments. Some succumbed to the difficulties, others became even more infused with their Light and ultimately transcended the suffering they were experiencing.

Now, I'm not asking you to ignore the suffering or the confusion. That might be impossible. But what I am asking you to consider is something I was unable to do. I'm asking you to continue **keeping your heart open,** even in the darkest moments, and I'm asking you to then **ask for help and keep asking for help.** That's all. You are not meant to do any of this time on Earth alone. We are here to help you and most certainly this loving Light is here to help you. But as you've known only too well, and as you've often shared with others, *first you must ask.* We can't help you until you ask. We know getting angrier and feeling badly often seems easier than asking for help because you are afraid the help won't come or be enough or do what you want it to do.

So, the question becomes for you to find out exactly what you want from the Light. Doesn't it? Well, what do you want? Do you want the Light to help make your life easier? Yes? Then I can promise you that will happen. I can promise you this.

But how do you want your life to become easier? That's the pivotal question. Because you see, whatever you envision as what will make life easier is probably going to only confuse you and limit your ability to open as fully as possible to letting this Light in.

Anything third-dimensional that you are expecting this Light to give you is going to totally negate what will actually be possible.

What will be possible? Well, that I can't tell you. That is something that you'll have to find out for yourself. Because how you respond to this Light as it totally fills your heart, soul, and spirit will be completely unique to you. *It's unique to everyone.* That is why the sages have never endeavored to describe this mystical experience. That is why they have said you will have to know it for yourself. Because it is totally between you and the Light that you can call God, the Light of Infinite Source, Brahma, whatever. The name doesn't matter. But the reason God as Brahma is never depicted is because it is indescribable and unknowable. It can only be experienced. And yes, you can experience it while you are alive. And then you will cease trying to manipulate your world the way you do now. There will no longer be a desire to do this. Nor a reason to care how others respond. It simply will no longer matter.

But **first you must let go**, Leia, and completely allow this to happen.

Yes, you've touched it. Yes, you've come mighty close. But no, you haven't completely surrendered yet. Not yet. But you will. And so will all the others who choose to read this. That is why you are reading this. To know once again, in this lifetime, that completely opening to the Light is possible for you.

Because you have all known this in other lifetimes. And now it is time to know it again.

• • • • • •

Chapter 15

Don't Have Any Expectations

From Linda:

After a rough start to the day and before I typed up Karampal's message filled with wisdom, Paul came through in our channeling session with a message that I hope he will share again here. He and K.P. don't share the same manner of speaking, but they certainly have the same ideas! Although some of what Paul says may seem shocking to those of us with delicate sensitivities, you can't miss the point.

From Paul:

Okay, so thank you once again for letting me tell my story about how we all get tripped up worrying about what other people will think. And we all do that. I know I did. Many times.

This whole conversation came about with you because you've been disappointed recently in how some in your family have responded to your honesty and open heart.

This has been pretty painful for you because you keep assuming that because you've changed, everyone else will be changing right along with you. And somehow this isn't quite turning out to be as you expected. People get stuck with an image of you and no matter what you may do or say, they most likely will keep that image pretty much until hell freezes over.

And the hypothesis that you thought we'd presented — as distilled in your mind — was that if you open and embrace your Light, then your universe will change and expand and everything will automatically be hunky dory with everyone all the time. Smooth sailing all the way home.

But... it's not turning out quite as you've expected. So, you are wondering why you're even bothering to give it all a go.

Now, this seems pretty silly to me after all the books you've written and all the hours of channeling and all the work you've done to help all these folks. But hope dies hard, doesn't it? Haven't given up how you think things ought to be for you to be okay.

And I offered you the example of how I really, really wanted to win an *Academy Award*. Oh God, how I wanted to be honored by everyone else and told how wonderful I was. And time after time, although I'd hit it out of the park, I was passed over. This was a bitter pill to swallow. When I was young and so in love with myself, I was sure that everyone else had to love me too. And lots of people said they did. But if there was a room full of adoring fans, and two people in the corner who didn't like me, then I was miserable. What was wrong with me? Didn't they see how wonderful I was?

So, that's how it went for a god-awful long time. I mean, I never really got over this. But it did drive me to try harder and do a better job.

See, life is a set up, my friend. And we are the ones who set it up. As I've said over and over: **we write the script.** Oh, you've heard that from other folks here too. Right.

Well, what I mean is that all those "nasty" people who are still not loving you the way you think they should now that your heart is "really open," may never take a different role in your play. And so what? What the hell difference does it make? Does this really change who you are?

So, all those years ago, I lusted after the *Oscar* and thought that was more important than anything. What was becoming President compared to that? Wasn't the *Oscar* the most important award anyone could possibly win? What was the *Nobel Peace prize* compared to that? *Any prize* for that matter. And this caused me to strive and struggle and just try to keep batting it out of the park. And I did it again and again. *"Paul Newman has done another Oscar-worthy performance."* And then I wouldn't win. So I'd chew some more nails and go after it again.

And then I won. I won. I did it. And they handed me this gold statue. I don't have it here at the moment or I'd show it to you. Matter of fact, I couldn't bring it with me. Nor could I bring any of the other awards I won all through the years. Nothing fit in my luggage when I was traveling here. Matter of fact, I got burned to bits [cremated], so it wouldn't have survived the heat anyway. I mean, don't you think it's funny that all those old pharaohs and what have you through the century got themselves buried with all their stuff?

Anyway, I won the award. And you know what I realized? It didn't change a thing. I mean, folks were now saying I was really, really *hot shit*. But there were still some folks who would rather have died than admitted that I deserved it. But now that didn't bother me so much because I'd realized that it didn't change me. I was still me. I still had to go to bed every night with me. Taking the *Oscar* to bed would have been uncomfortable. And of course, *Joanne* didn't think I was any different. And neither did my kids. They said they were happy for me.

But I still had to take a piss and get into bed. Just me. Same old body, same old guy.

So, what was that all about, anyway? Did it change anything about my life? Am I better for winning? Was I better for striving to do my best?

You see, when you are young and everything gets handed to you, you never actually appreciate anything. But when you struggle to achieve stuff and really pull stuff out of yourself, then you do appreciate everything a lot more.

The same is true about this Light we keep talking about. It's always been in you and everything else around you. But you've never really appreciated it because you've always had it. I was always a good actor. Always had talent. But I never appreciated it until I heard other people telling me I was good and even then that wasn't enough.

So, we keep telling you that you and Martin have a lot of Light. And other people tell you that too. You've won the equivalent of the *Oscar* a few times already. But it's never been enough.

Just like winning the *Oscar* wasn't enough for me. Why?

Because you still don't love yourself enough regardless of what anyone else thinks.

I mean, **it really doesn't matter what anyone else thinks.** And until you've gotten to that place, this plan isn't going to work.

There is only one source that has an opinion that really matters. And that's been inside you all along. One source. And you can call it whatever you want, but it's the same amazing Light that has created everything and loves everything that you can see. And until you just focus on that, and let that in, you will continue to be disappointed by what happens there on Earth.

Hell, a lot of folks are afraid now. A lot of folks are confused. A lot of folks don't know which way is "up." So having expectations of how they may respond to the Light flowing from you may not be a really good idea. I mean, actually having *any* expectations about *anything* might not be a really good idea. I had expectations about how I'd feel after winning the Oscar and boy, was I disappointed! I'm suggesting the same may be true for you here.

Don't have any expectations, but do know that letting this Light flow through in full force will be better than anything you or I or anyone could experience on that little blue ball. This beats it all. Really. You're gonna have to trust that. Because it's true.

•• •• ••

Chapter 16

Laugh at Yourself to Weaken the Ego's Grip

From Linda:

I keep discovering so many ways to trip myself up here. In our channeling session today with the *Ascended Master El Morya Khan,* he did offer some comfort. He is telling us that as the frequencies of transformation are increasing on the Earth plane, our ego selves which are fueled by our karmic history, are having a stronger grip, an iron grip on running our lives. I can attest to this! I became furious yesterday as I was preparing food to take to a joint holiday celebration with friends. My family, especially Martin, was not behaving as I thought they should. Never mind how I was behaving!

I can't believe that I can accomplish all I think I must do each day without engaging my ego mind. And yet, we are assured that once we completely shift consciousness to this omniscient Light that we carry within, we can handle all the stresses of this world with even greater ease. Really?

From Karampal:

Of course you have our sympathy, Leia, as you move through this enormous challenge of awakening while you still have a body. We know. We know. We continue to tell you we know because we would still love to let our egos take over even here. We'd love to, but we can't. We know that even our desire to collaborate with you could be ego-driven. But we are going with the idea that this is our karmic agreement with you. And, oh yes, karma can be an ego-driven construct. You know that only too well.

But the difference may be that we are doing this completely in service to the Light. A rededication, if you will, in every moment to simply being expressions of this enormously loving Light that is filling our beings now. We don't want to walk away from this.

And anytime we even feel a glimmer of ego, it plunges us into such dark despair that it separates us from this Light. We simply don't want that. The Light keeps us honest.

We know we feel differently to you than if we were at the level of the beings of Light with whom you normally connect. But we are trying to "keep our hand in," stay more accessible to you so you will know that we are offering as immediate and comprehensible a perspective as we possibly can to all that is going on with you there.

So, what you are truly interested in understanding now is more of the "mechanics" of this whole idea. You are still connecting with *Yogananda's* teachings as well and understand the pivotal idea of the *kundalini* energy rising up the spine to facilitate this complete embrace of this Light by your physical form.

If I were to tell you that all the emotional discomfort you are choosing to experience now is a result of this energy rising in your spine, would you choose to believe this? The more intense the discomfort, the more rapid the influx of this Light is becoming to fill your form.

Now, we know this may not be comforting news to you. Why would it be? But again, this is nothing that is "happening" to you. **This is something you are co-creating** because your agenda and the agenda of everyone there is to completely embrace this Light, one way or another. You get to choose how that will be accomplished. *Will you choose grace and ease or suffering?* This is where your Divine Will comes into play.

Now, we can stand on the sidelines, as we often do and give you warnings. We give you plenty of those. And as soon as you get uncomfortable, you know what's going on.

But this "iron grip" of the ego mind is no exaggeration. It really does not want to let go. We can see that. And as *El Morya Khan* said, it is a universal challenge. You aren't the only ones going through this by any stretch of the imagination. It's gotten worse even since I was there. Much worse. It seems as if your world continues to go mad.

Which is why you are hearing to **have even more compassion** and **open your heart to loving self even more fully** as you go through this time.

And this is why we are here to help you now and aid you in spreading the word to as many as will listen to what you are learning here. Let the word out. It needs to be shared.

So, of course we will tell you, once again, that **you must sit and meditate every day** and as often as possible every day as you can. Go within. Go within. Go within. We know this is getting more difficult than ever before because of this iron grip of the ego mind. It is a challenge. We understand.

Here is what we suggest that you do about this. As soon as your mind wanders from opening your heart and focus on your Light, **we want you to laugh at yourself.** Yes, laugh at yourself. Think of what serious thoughts are confusing and worrying you and think of them as being very, very funny. Because once you get here and look at all the thoughts that cluttered your mind, you will find that most of them were very silly and unnecessary. Unbelievable what humans clutter their minds with by worrying. Unbelievable. And yet, when you really let these thoughts take hold, all this incredible worry and fear, it does have a grip on you and leads to all sorts of suffering if you allow it. This is why the thought of laughing at this energy seems so strange to you. But **when you laugh, you must open your heart and it will diffuse the energy that is gripping you.** Energetically this is the most effective technique for destroying the ego's grip. If you decide your mind is behaving in a silly manner, it must give up the game.

And Paul and I do think these worries and fears are silly. We really do.

Once you surrender to this Light, you will only be able to manifest a Light-filled universe in which to reside. You will only be able to respond to any event with an unconditionally loving heart. All else will be impossible. Just impossible.

So, as you begin to open your heart in meditation, let your heart help you laugh at what is troubling you. No need for self abnegation or punishment. No reason for this. You see, **laughter is a form of compassion, a form of self love.** Then just keep thinking of this beautiful Light that is filling your heart, soul, and spirit. Let it diffuse throughout your form.

Let it fill your spine, legs, and arms. Float away on a sea of Light. Be washed away by it.

Be enfolded in it. Let it nurture your whole body. If another thought of fear or pain arises, laugh it away as you become completely engulfed in your Light.

What a wondrous experience to accept and allow what is already in you to flow through you. We can help you do this. Each time you feel even the least bit stuck, we can help you laugh about it. We both know how silly we were. We can help you see how silly you are!

Then we ask you to **trust that as you open and fully allow this Light in, it will take care of you and carry you through this time of awakening.** This Light is filling creation to preserve and enhance it, not to destroy it. It is the ego consciousness of humans that is the creator of destructive thoughts. This never, ever comes from the Light. This is absolutely the truth.

So, when you allow this Light to completely fill you, it will nurture you completely. That is all it is designed to do. There is no other program for it. Let if fill your spine. Let it fill your body. Let it fill your soul. And laugh at yourself as you do this. We will be laughing with joy as you allow this to happen.

•• •• ••

Chapter 17

Lifting the Veil of Forgetfulness

From Linda:

K.P.'s plan seems to have been a good one for me. Each time my mind began to wander from the Light as I moved through the day, I'd remember to laugh at whatever I was thinking, and immediately I'd re-center and be back allowing my Light to help me with whatever task was at hand.

Then, during my early morning meditation, as I once again was feeling challenged to center in my Light, I began to laugh inwardly at whatever thoughts were occupying my mind. Immediately, I was able to open to my Light and begin a meditation that allowed the *kundalini* energy at the tip of my spine to rise. It came in powerfully and sent me out into the universe where I revisited an early vision of three luminous pyramids floating through space. At the time of this vision, nearly twenty years ago, I had been so taken with it that I had not allowed a complete message regarding this vision to come through. I only allowed myself to understand that a pyramid could be invoked prior to opening to meditation, Light work, or channeling and this would be a harmonious force field to utilize.

Now, I was seeing that these three pyramids, each a bit

different in the colors of Light filling them, were actually the energy force fields that house the Higher Selves of K.P., of Martin, and of me. And when we entered the Earth plane as a group, this is how we traveled here initially. Then I saw that everyone and every living thing on this planet has the same pyramid construct with which they are connected.

This is apparently why, through the ages, the pyramid has been constructed as a sacred space out of three-dimensional matter. So, now I see everyone as carrying around this pyramid that is housing their Light.

I also saw an image of my eldest son as an infant completely filled with a blazing Light. This was very healing for me karmically. We have been repeatedly told that the strongest karmic link we have on the Earth plane is between mother and child. As this *kundalini* energy rose within me in my meditation, any disharmony in the karma with my son was also cleared. Amazing stuff. Just keep laughing, right?

Here's Paul again:

Okay, Linda. I see you are getting to some really meaty stuff. Glad we've been able to help.

I know I don't fit directly into the picture of you and Karampal and Martin coming here on the same stream of Light. But that's okay. I had my own group that came in together. And I'm working with them too.

Being able to travel back and forth to see where we began and where we are going has been incredibly exhilarating and fascinating for me. When you go to the Earth, you forget just about everything. It's rather sad to see how — if only I'd understood it all a bit better — I would have done so many things differently. This *Veil of Forgetfulness* is very real. Few people get to penetrate it, and when they do it without understanding what they are getting into it can literally drive someone crazy. A lot of the folks you do call crazy there are folks who are getting a part of the picture but don't know how to handle the information. You need to have some wisdom and understanding to handle this information without going nuts.

That is why there were always secret schools where you could learn some of this stuff, but not a general training where everything could be learned. The Buddhists do it as well as about anybody on Earth right now.

Hell, the *Vatican* knows it all and has known it all for centuries. But they don't want everyone to know it for many reasons. Some of those reasons seem like a good idea, because some of the power that would be possible for everyone could be used to destroy everything by unprincipled people. That is why *Hitler* was after all this information. The *Vatican* knew that and did try to keep him at bay and confuse him instead of teach him anything really valuable.

All through the ages there have been unprincipled people who have tried to know what is easily available now and have caused all sorts of problems with what they've learned. That was why, after *Atlantis* sank because of a misuse of this information, the *Veil of Forgetfulness* was put in place more fully.

Earth entered the *Dark Ages* from which it is just emerging now.

Meanwhile, without the knowledge of the Light, destruction has still occurred. Unprincipled people are in the Vatican too, and have been for centuries withholding crucial information that could really help so they could keep the power over people.

But you see, **that is all dying away now.** It has to. That's because the Light is flooding the planet and cleaning all that stuff out. Everything on Earth is coming to Light.

And if someone wants to use this power in a destructive way, they will destroy themselves first. It's just the way it is now. If your heart isn't truly open while you are learning this info and you use the energy in a not so kind way, you'll know it right away. It will feel terrible. Well, yes, I guess you've both tested that theory there, right?

Now, I can't say whether any of this is good or bad or right or wrong. I get that. I can't take sides. I can only tell you what I see and let you know that none of it is wrong. It's all this karma stuff that is working itself out for everybody.

But **the sooner you get over judging all this history, and judging anything, the easier it will be for you.** Let this Light rise up and fill you fully, and then as you learn stuff, just feel free to share it. It's time for it all to come out.

And we've agreed to help you do that. If someone misuses

what they learn here to try to have power over anyone else, that trip will end quickly.

If they open and allow all this stuff to heal them and truly open their hearts to this glorious Light (don't have words to describe the indescribable), they won't even want to harm anyone else. They will just want to share this Light and *be this Light* as they walk around there.

So, don't worry about how this will affect others. Just share what you know.

There's a good girl. You too, Martin. You're doing your job well now.

I know, I know. You want me to tell you **what I see in the future.** I've let that cat out of the bag again, haven't I?

So, let me explain this as well as I can.

You know that this whole universe is made up of a multitude of dimensions, right? You know all that quantum physics/metaphysical stuff. And these dimensions also include possible scenarios, dreams, stories, movies, imaginative things, you name it. It's all there. Anything that's had a lot of folks thinking about it has then gone from this possible scenario to a probable scenario and then if enough folks think about it, it becomes an event there. Didn't you write about this in one of your books?[3]

Okay, so you see there are a few different ways things can go there. We see all these different streams flowing out from

---

[3] Paul is referring to *Affirmations and Thought Forms* published by Expansion Publishing; www.expansionpublishing.com.

folks' consciousness. Remember, you all co-create what you will experience there.

So, there's a bunch of folks who think this is "end times" and are sending a lot of power to those thoughts. Then there's a bunch of folks who think the whole Earth will move to a higher dimension because of the force field the Earth has entered now. Then there's folks who think that your planet is in the process of waking up and healing itself from the destructive stuff that humans have done to it. And then there's folks who look at the history of Earth and see that we've been on a very long honeymoon as a human race, and that our time might just be over on that planet.

Some folks think some guys from space or some Archangels will come down and rescue a "chosen few" when that scene or one of those other scenes happen. 144,000. Right?

So, let me ask you this. What do you think will really happen? Got the picture?

Now this is what I can honestly tell you. **Whatever you think it is that will happen is exactly what will happen for you.**

This you can trust.

Gotcha there, didn't I?

Let me give you some graphic examples of what I mean here. Let's use you, here and now, for an example.

You and Martin are living in a gorgeous part of the Earth. It's spectacular there. No one can deny that, nor should they.

It's fertile; the weather isn't too bad most of the time. Lots of sun, and you love that. Your house is not too shabby. In fact, many folks would say that's spectacular too. The economy is good. You have plenty to eat, plenty to wear. You and Martin have a pretty good marriage. Your health is good. See what I'm getting at? You're doing okay, aren't you?

Yet, not all the folks around you there are doing quite as well as the two of you. In fact, you know for a fact that many folks are struggling either emotionally, physically, or both.

So, let's enlarge the picture. Let's look at this thing globally. You all live on the same planet, but would you say that, as you look around the planet there are that many people living the way the two of you do? In fact, are many more not doing quite as well, and some really badly? Is that possible to say? Yet, you are all living on the same planet at the same time.

But tonight, as you go to bed will you be worrying about whether you can feed your family tomorrow, or the next day? I doubt it. Unless you decide to go to that dimension of lack and take that particular universe on. Choice is yours of course.

Now, we are not saying that you are superior to the folks who are currently living on other dimensions on your planet. It's all karmic. You know that. You've just chosen to heal a heckuva lot of karma and chose to come in with the tools to do that. Not good or bad, right or wrong. It just is. That's all. But you get my point. You've all agreed to be on that little blue ball rolling around in space at this amazing time. But **you are on different dimensions already.**

Now, where do you want to go from here? You've written a book about this.[4]

This is what I would suggest. Just do the healing work and open to your Light and simply trust that whatever happens, it will be perfect for you. Because it will.

When will it happen? It's already happening. Just open, keep healing and letting this Light flow through you. You are already on your way.

•• •• ••

---

[4] *Navigating the Fourth Dimension,* www.expansionpublishing.com.

Epilogue

Unmasking the Ego's Tricks

By Martin Luthke

We have read in these chapters that the ego mind has an iron grip on all of us. Even Paul and K.P. admit that they are not entirely free from ego temptations – and that giving in to them inevitably results in deep despair. Thus, it is fair to say that the ego is a formidable obstacle to anyone's happiness.

Before we look more closely at the tricks of the ego that get in the way of our happiness, a brief **definition of the "ego mind"** may be in order: The ego is an instrument of our own making that serves the Veil of Forgetfulness. Its origins are rooted in collective and individual karma. The ego is not wrong or bad but it does create an obstacle to happiness and a full embodiment and expression of one's Light. The ego is rooted in the illusions of separation and control. It operates out of ignorance and feeds on fears and desires. It has "a mind of its own" and is primarily interested in its own power and self-importance; it wants to be right, even if it kills us. The ego will inevitably tell you that it has your highest good at heart, is serving your needs, and is protecting you from harm. We all fall for this "sales pitch" and grant it control over much of our thought processes and emotional experiences. (In a sense it is like "malware" hijacking our computers.) The fact is, we do not need the ego to be happy or safe – our own unobstructed Light does a very fine job providing for all our needs, our joys, and our safety if only our egos were to get out of the way.

What then are some of the tricks that the ego employs to keep us from embodying our Light more fully? Without claiming completeness, I shall briefly discuss four major tricks:

(1)   Moving out of the Here and Now

(2)   Creating Self-fulfilling Prophecies

(3)   Setting up Conditions of Happiness

(4)   Setting up the Self-Improvement Trap

Moving Out of the Here and Now

Our Totalities (or Higher Selves) contain all that we are, all that we have ever been, and all that we will ever be. Our Totalities exist in the Eternal Now, unlimited by third-dimensional constraints of time and space. When we focus on the Here and Now – the present time and space – we can align ourselves more easily with the frequencies of our Totalities. When we allow our ego minds to focus on the past or the future (which are constructs or projections that exist only in our minds), we create a misalignment with our Totalities.

Focusing on the past we invite regrets, remorse, depression, or generally a longing for a state that is no longer (and may never have been). Focusing on the future we invite worry and fear, or generally a longing for a state that is different from the one we are in (and may never be). Those thoughts and feelings take us away from being fully present, alive, and inserted in the Here and Now.

You may ask, "Why is it wrong to enjoy pleasant memories of the past or anticipate joy in the future?" Of course, there is nothing wrong with using our ego minds in this fashion. But we are paying a hefty price: When we reminisce we add to the flavor of our "sweet memories" the bitter realization that the good old times are no longer. When we experience pleasant sensations in anticipation of future joy we automatically generate fear that those gratifying moments may not come to pass; we also set ourselves up for disappointment when the actual experience does not match the built-up expectations.

True untainted joy can only be experienced in the Here and Now. You cannot hold on to it, you cannot anticipate it. It is – not it was or *will be*. The ego sweet-talks us into accepting a "deal": Trading memories or expectations for the experience of true joy. Many of us are so lost in our mental spaces and times that we wouldn't recognize opportunities for joy right here, right now, if they clubbed us over the head. And if we don't recognize such opportunities to feel joyful then we would certainly not feel gratitude for our blessings – once more depriving ourselves of additional benefits that come with the experience of gratitude.

Creating Self-fulfilling Prophecies

In the preceding chapters we have read repeatedly that we are co-creating our experiences with our thoughts – continuously.[5] This is one of the truths the ego doesn't want us to know, for it is the outcome of the ego's thoughts that the ego uses to justify its existence and supremacy. For instance, the ego dwells on thoughts of future lack. This sets in motion a process which actually manifests lack. Then the ego tells us, "I told you so. There is reason to be afraid of lack and you better listen to my advice and allow me to guard you against lack in the future." And if we do, lack will, indeed, be in our future, thus reinforcing the ego's iron grip!

Fear begets fear. The ego can be compared to the monsters in the animated movie *Monster, Inc.* which depend for their energetic survival on the screams of frightened children. If only we didn't allow our egos to scare us by monstrous thoughts of our own making!

Setting up Conditions of Happiness

Another trick of the ego is tying our happiness to conditions. "I can only be happy if [fill in the condition]" or conversely, "I cannot be happy as long as [fill in the condition]." This all makes perfect sense to our ego minds. There are two problems, however. Such thinking denies our sovereignty and makes us dependent on conditions which may very well be out of our

[5]   More about that in Affirmations and Thought Forms; www.expansionpublishing.com.

control. It sets us up to feel victimized by life, bitter, and angry. Of course, sometimes it "works," we satisfy a condition and feel momentarily happy. Psychologists call this "intermittent reinforcement" which makes us try over and over again.

Then the ego moves the goalposts and sets up another condition: *I can only be happy if... Susie loves me... I graduate from school... I get a job... I marry Susie... I own a home... I have kids... I get a raise... I divorce Susie... I sell the home... and so on until I reach retirement. Then my prostate troubles me and my joints ache... "and then you die."*

We allow the ego to cheat us out of our happiness. Most of us chase our happiness like the dog which has a sausage dangling in front of his nose that is tied to a harness strapped around his neck. No matter how fast we run, we never quite catch it, or at least not for long. As children we know that happiness can be unconditional; with the ascendancy of the ego, we forget this truth.

Setting up the Self-Improvement Trap

A variation of the third trick discussed above is what I call the self-improvement trap. What could be wrong with self-improvement? Didn't our parents, teachers, coaches, mentors, therapists, pastors/priests/rabbis and gurus all advocate self-improvement? Don't we *know* we should lose weight, exercise or meditate more, floss regularly, take our vitamins, become more productive or a better parent or spouse, give more to charity, be kinder, wiser, more loving, considerate, virtuous? Of course! The trouble is – and I have tried this program for 55 years – it doesn't make you happy!

This program is a variation on the "conditions of happiness," only that most of these conditions are internal and hard to observe. This allows our ego to move the goalposts even more randomly, and our inner critic to lash out at us even more harshly and unreasonably. And if we judge ourselves we tend to judge others as well – and then live in fear of their judgments.

No matter how hard we try, if we strive to improve ourselves we will never end up loving ourselves. Why? Because if we consider ourselves in need of improvement we implicitly judge and reject ourselves. What you resist, persists. And so the knot tightens.

The Masters have stated repeatedly: *No one is broken, no one needs fixing.* Falling into the self-improvement trap denies this truth. As Paul and K.P. stated in the preceding chapters, success or failure, vice or virtue are irrelevant on the higher planes. The only question that counts is *how much Light you carry within.* The Light loves and accepts us *as we are,* why second-guess it?

Why should I exhaust myself in endless self-improvement efforts, only to feel frustrated with the results, angry at the demands for perfection, and an utter failure? Would Buddha have gained enlightenment if he had been concerned with improving his Body Mass Index? Isn't it wiser and more compassionate to accept – and laugh about – my body and personality cloak that I have chosen this time around? After all, it is just a mask, a persona. Isn't it truly liberating to realize that the Light *doesn't care* whether you are a "good" or "improved" person, only whether you love yourself?

So, the next time you fall for any of your ego's tricks – and you will in short order – forgive yourself, feel compassion, and love yourself – including this pesky ego of yours.

•• •• •• •• •• ••

Appendix A

Introduction to Psychoenergetic Healing

If you are interested in doing the work of personal transformation and healing suggested throughout this book, you may be interested in an innovative form of therapy we have called *Psychoenergetic* Healing.

Searching for Better Ways

Can you imagine the practice of medicine before the invention of X-ray machines or microscopes? Would you want to refer someone to a doctor who refuses to consider anything that is not visible to the naked eye? The field of psychotherapy, as it is taught in graduate school today, can be likened to the practice of medicine based on a 19th-century view of the world. While there are many fine, traditionally-trained psychotherapists out there, psychotherapy is still very much a "hit or miss" endeavor.

We propose that the practice of psychotherapy (and healing in general) cannot advance significantly without a shift in paradigm, i.e., a fundamental reorientation. Within the established paradigm there is no convincing explanation for phenomena such as the placebo effect, "spontaneous" remissions, psychosomatic illnesses, "miracle cures," healing through prayer or touch, etc. As long as the premises of the healing arts are based on a material or mental - rather than energetic - understanding of reality, their efforts resemble attempts to assemble a million-piece puzzle without an idea of the larger picture. In the final analysis, scientific "progress" based on a misunderstanding is like getting better at "barking up the wrong tree."

Psychoenergetic Healing is based on a "new" paradigm that is compatible with ancient wisdom teachings as well as modern sciences. Leading-edge physicists have now come to insights similar to those of ancient mystics: All there is, all matter and all of Creation, is "patterned" energy, vibrating to specific frequencies that distinguish one manifestation of energy from another.

What is Psychoenergetic Healing?

All psychological manifestations, such as thoughts, feelings, and behavior patterns, are also "patterned" energy. Effective psychological healing, regardless of the method or technique, occurs when there is a change in the basic energies that charge our feelings, thoughts, memories and habits. While all psychotherapeutic methods are intended to produce such healing, most do not target the energetic level directly.

Psychoenergetic Healing takes into account the fact that human beings are not only physical, emotional, and mental beings, but also, and most essentially, spiritual beings. This truth is not a mere statement of faith; it can be experienced in a direct, tangible manner. No matter what names or interpretations we prefer, a spiritual, healing energy, or Light, can be accessed by all human beings regardless of our belief systems and can be utilized effectively for healing on all levels.

The practitioner of Psychoenergetic Healing uses a variety of techniques that affect the mental and emotional energies on a fundamental level, thus going directly to the source of the individual's discomfort. While going to the core of the matter may be a frightening thought to many, it is actually a very healing, safe, efficient, and effective method that does not require the unbuffered reliving of traumatic memories or painful feelings.

What Happens in a Typical Session?

What happens in a session is very much guided by the individual's issues and needs, making each session a unique experience. Most sessions include elements of traditional "talking therapy," expanded upon with work performed in an altered state of consciousness we call "Inner Space" where the client can experience the richness of his or her multidimensional nature. Facilitated by the therapist, the client achieves a heightened state of consciousness in which he or she may become aware of colors, images, thoughts, memories, feelings, or physical sensations, such as pain, heat, weight, etc. The range of experiences in Inner Space is virtually unlimited and may include an awareness of past lives, other dimensions, the presence of beings of Light, and more.

While each client has a different experience, all are able to perceive the flow of energies within. These inner perceptions then guide the course of the healing work. Using what could be called a "psychological X-ray technique," the client can become aware of the core issue and then observe the process of healing on an energetic level as it is occurring. Although getting in touch with painful feelings or experiences may cause some temporary discomfort, an energetic shift and tangible relief can often be felt within minutes. Because the client has control over his or her Inner Space and all therapeutic interventions are guided by the client's inner perceptions, this approach to healing is experienced as empowering and safe.

Who Can Benefit From Psychoenergetic Healing?

Our experience has shown that Psychoenergetic Healing can be an effective approach regardless of the presenting problem, as all thoughts, memories, feelings, and habits exist as "patterned" energies and can be treated as such. Psychoenergetic Healing has been successfully applied to a wide variety of issues, including anger, fear, depression, addictions, sexual issues, co-dependency, low self-esteem, traumatic experiences, psychosomatic illnesses, pain, grieving and loss, etc. Clients of all ages, including children and adolescents, have benefited greatly from Psychoenergetic Healing, regardless of their belief systems or prior experience with energy-based healing.

Most of us are not consciously aware of the subtle energies that fuel our behaviors and states of mind at all times, and yet we all have noticed emotional energies in action, such as when we experience intense anger, fear, or resentment. If we do not release and balance negative emotions properly, but instead "sweep them under the rug," they may linger in our emotional body for an unlimited time, causing further disturbance. They may even manifest in physical disease. To gain or maintain a state of harmony and health, it is essential to attend to emotional disharmonies, resolve inner conflicts, and release traumatic memories.

Many of our clients have already accomplished a significant amount of inner work, be it emotional or spiritual in nature, and desire to further their growth by addressing those issues that previously seemed intractable. Thus, to benefit from Psychoenergetic Healing, a commitment to growth can be more relevant than the nature of the problem or whether it fits into any traditional diagnostic pigeonhole.

For more information on Psychoenergetic Healing as well as on how to become a Psychoenergetic Healer, please visit *www.u-r-light*.com or read ***Beyond Psychotherapy.***

•• •• ••

Appendix B

Publications from Expansion Publishing

Expansion Publishing is offering additional titles by Linda Stein-Luthke and Martin F. Luthke, Ph.D.:

AGREEMENTS. Lessons I Chose on My Journey toward the Light, by Linda Stein-Luthke, ISBN 978-0-9656927-7-9, 338 pp. E-Book: US$9.99. This captivating narrative tells the story of the life and adventures of a "western" woman with "eastern" experiences. Told with candor and humility, it describes the agony and ecstasy of an exceptional growth process that includes fascinating encounters with many Masters on this and the higher planes. The reader will come away inspired and encouraged to seek the personal relationship to the Light that weaves like a common thread through the author's ongoing journey toward awakening. More than an interesting autobiography, AGREEMENTS is thus a "teaching tale" with a universal message.

Balancing the Light Within. A Discourse on Healing from the Ascended Master St. Germain, by Linda Stein-Luthke and Martin F. Luthke, ISBN 0-9656927-0-1, 54 pp. Book: US$6.95; E-Book: US$3.99. A channeled discourse on light vibrations, tools of awareness, chakras, healing of self and others with metaphysical means; suggested readings.

Affirmations and Thought Forms: *You Can Change Your Mind! A Discourse from the Ascended Master St. Germain,* by Linda Stein-Luthke and Martin F. Luthke, ISBN 0-9656927-1-X, 48 pp. Book: US$6.95; E-Book: US$3.99. A channeled discourse on the use of affirmations and the power of thought forms and how to use both for healing purposes, with emphasis on self-empowerment and self-awareness; suggested readings.

Angels and Other Beings of Light: *They are Here to Help You! A Discourse from the Ascended Master St. Germain,* by Linda Stein-Luthke and Martin F. Luthke, ISBN 0-9656927-3-6, 84 pp. Book: US$8.95; E-Book: US$4.99. A channeled discourse on working with angels, Archangels, Ascended Masters, Twin Flame, soul mates, and other beings of Light; who they are; what their purpose is; how to contact them; how to experience your Higher Self; suggested readings.

Navigating the Fourth Dimension: *A Discourse from the Ascended Masters St. Germain and El Morya Khan,* by Linda Stein-Luthke and Martin F. Luthke, ISBN 0-9656927-5-2, 134 pp. Book: US$11.95; E-Book: US$6.99. A channeled discourse explaining why the past no longer applies and proposing new ways of thinking, being and creating that can lead to an experience of harmony, balance, peace and abundance in the here and now. The appendix contains the first ten issues of the Ascended Masters Newsletter.

Dispelling the Illusions of Aging and Dying:
A Discourse from the Ascended Master St. Germain. By
Linda Stein-Luthke & Martin F. Luthke, ISBN 0-9656927-6-
0, 90 pp. Book: US$11.95; E-Book: US$6.99. The two greatest
fears that human beings possess are the fears of aging and
dying — and that is exactly what holds you in the grip of the
process of aging and dying. This book helps you to realize
that every fear you have is illusory. When you move beyond
the five senses, you can see these illusions for yourself. — If
you choose to follow the suggestions offered by the Ascended
Master St. Germain and heal your fears, you will move into a
greater awareness of the only true reality there is: that all is
Light — and that includes you.

Beyond Psychotherapy: *Introduction to Psychoenergetic Healing,* by Martin F. Luthke and Linda Stein-
Luthke, ISBN 0-9656927-4-4, 228 pp. Book: US$19.95; E-
Book: US$9.99. This book by the founders of Psychoenergetic
Healing describes an advanced approach to the healing
of emotional, mental, spiritual and physical issues. A
groundbreaking introduction for healers, psycho-therapists
and all who are interested in energy-based healing methods.

Riding the Tide of Change: *Preparing for Personal
& Planetary Transformation,* by Martin F. Luthke, ISBN
0-9656927-2-8, 108 pp. Book: US$9.95; E-Book: US$5.99.
A metaphysical book on Earth changes with an emphasis
on releasing fears, healing self, and understanding our role
as co-creators during this time of transformation; suggested
readings.

Ascended Masters Newsletters Volume I – V, by Linda Stein-Luthke and Martin F. Luthke, E-Book: US$3.99 each. These volumes are a compilation of Ascended Masters News-letters in form of an E-book, offering valuable information and guidance for our times.

How to Order

For more information: For more information and secure on-line orders, please visit *www. expansionpublishing.com.* You may e-mail any inquiries to *expansion@u-r-light.com.* Please contact us for quantity discounts.

For on-line orders of book, e-books, and audio files: Please visit *www.expansionpublishing.com.*

Bookstores: All printed books are also available through your local bookstore. However, you may need to special-order them.

How to Contact the Authors

Linda and Martin welcome your comments and are available for workshops, seminars, and individual sessions (also by phone). Inquiries and correspondence should be directed to *expansion@u-r-light.com.*

FREE Ascended Masters Newsletter

Periodically, we offer a free newsletter with channeled information from the Ascended Masters as well as updates about our work, trainings, and publications. Please visit *www. expansionpublishing.com* and click on *Ascended Masters Newsletter* for details.

.. ..

CPSIA information can be obtained
at www.ICGtesting.com
Printed in the USA
LVOW04s1439110716
495866LV00046B/1084/P